THE POWER
of
Now
IN YOUR LIFE

Tangela B. Pierce

MORGAN JAMES PUBLISHING • NEW YORK

THE POWER of Now IN YOUR LIFE

Copyright ©2007 Tangela Pierce

ISBN: 1-60037-186-8 (Paperback)

Published by:

MORGAN · JAMES
THE ENTREPRENEURIAL PUBLISHER ™
www.morganjamespublishing.com

Morgan James Publishing, LLC
1225 Franklin Ave Ste 32
Garden City, NY 11530-1693
Toll Free 800-485-4943
www.MorganJamesPublishing.com

Cover Design by:
James & Linder Hunn
VMPublications@yahoo.com

Interior Design by:
Rachel Campbell
rcampbell77@cox.net

Habitat for Humanity®
Peninsula
Building Partner

PowerOf NowNTan.com
Or Write: Tangela B. Pierce
5007C Victory Blvd Suite 159 • Yorktown, Va 23693

Dedication

I WOULD LIKE TO DEDICATE this book to the men and women who have loved, trained and stood by me, my husband and family when the gates of hell came against us. God blessed us with a host of angels who spoke into our lives at some critical times. It was the standard of the Lord instilled by these Pastors and Teachers. Your training and prayers preserved us and stopped hell's plan of destruction. God used each of you to love and train us while pointing to our destiny.

Apostle Sammy C. Smith & 1ˢᵗ Lady Violet

Pastor Geoff Dudley & 1ˢᵗ Lady Glenda

Bishop Steven W. Banks & Pastor Keira

Pastors Dorothy & Lawrence Govan

Dr's David & Vernette Rosier

Each of you stood on the wall and watched for our souls as we sought the Lord............

And he sought God in the days of Zechariah, who had understanding in the visions of God: and as long as he sought the Lord, God made him to prosper.   2 Chronicles 26:5

Acknowledgements

I WOULD LIKE TO THANK my many spiritual fathers and mother who spoke into my spirit man.

Bishop TD Jakes

Bishop Eddie Long

Dr Myles Monroe

Pastor Creflo Dollar

Joyce Meyers

Thank you from your unknown spiritual daughter and thousands like me. We recognize God's breath moving across your anointed vocal cords. You taught us how to become an instrument fit for the Master's use. When that breath was released, the sound of God's voice transcended through many dimensions to find us. Our hearing became sharpened while in the darkest seasons of our lives. This gave us the ability to hear past the noises of life that were trying to silence one of the most powerful tools God has given to us…**Hearing**. Once our hearing was restored, we regained our ability to speak life in our "NOWs." Your daughters of many faces, nationalities and religious backgrounds would like to say THANK YOU. Thank you for all your tireless teaching, preaching, and book writing for it has fallen on good ground. God bless you.

Your Unknown Spiritual Daughter

(& many others like me)

Tangela

V

Thank You So Much

A SPECIAL THANKS TO MY editor, Adria Strothers. God used your divine grammatical touch to make this into a masterpiece.

A special thanks to my cover designer, Elders James & Linder Hunn. You took my ideas and made them a reality.

A special thanks to my kids, Omari, Marquita and Demetrius. You loved me through the process of time and released me to finish this project.

A special thanks to my husband Caleb. Words cannot express what you mean to me. Thank you for all your help with the computer, editing, research and spelling words day in and day out. You helped me put God's vision for this book into words. God's plan brought you into my life and you loved me into my NOW. You patiently helped me put my story together. Thank you babe...........I literally could not have done this without you!

Table of Contents

Foreword

THE POWER OF "NOW" IN *Your Life* is a must read for the body of Christ. It is a practical easy to read book that will enhance the lives of those who read it. Many in the body of Christ are stuck in situations and need to understand that they are doing the same things over and over again which got them into their present situation.

Our own words can create a world for us that can be life or death. What is happening to us right now is a direct harvest of what we planted last season. The body of Christ is going through an identity crisis. We really don't know who we are. Therefore, we are unable to be used by God to express His image on earth. We are unable to rule and reign because we do not know who we are.

The bible says we should be able to comfort others with the comfort we have received from God. Tangela has put her life in a book to bring life to others.

We have known the author for some time now and can see the words in this book made flesh in her life. This book is not just another book to read but real life that can bring change to those that will read it. As you read this book expect your faith to go to another level that you may experience the power of "Now."

This book will help those that are procrastinators. Within the word "procrastinate" we have the word "castrate." Many people are cutting off their future by not operating in the now.

We highly recommend this book for those who are tired of things as usual and those who are ready to step into their blessed place in God.

Drs. David & Vernette Rosier
Fellowship Church of Praise
Network of Covenant Churches and Ministries
Apostolic Overseers

AS I BEGAN TO READ "The Power of "NOW" in Your Life, I believe this to be a work of the Holy Spirit. It is a book for this hour, for those who are ready to move to the next dimension of transformation. **Information** leads to **revelation,** which results in **transformation.**

God has given Tangela this revelation of "NOW" after experiencing and overcoming many challenges and obstacles in her life. NOW is when your humanity collides with divinity resulting in your destiny, or in other words, when kairos invades chronos. What a powerful revelation! We should SEEK to UNDERSTAND and EMBRACE this thought provoking concept of the power of NOW.

From the pages of this book, your mind will be renewed, and will thrust you into a new realm of understanding your purpose and destination. I like what Tan wrote. "Each NOW of your life is the hope of a beginning." When you change your life, you change your destination. DISCOVER YOUR "NOW" LIFESTYLE.... NOW.

Apostle Sammy C. Smith
Pastor and Founder
Grace Cathedral Ministries
Sumter, South Carolina

Introduction

ADAM, WHERE ARE YOU..... "NOW"?

IN ONE OF MY MANY YEARS OF DEPRESSION, God asked me this question, "*What is "now?*" I paused long enough to listen to the question, meaning I stopped the noise within myself to try to comprehend what God was really asking me? In that hesitation of uncertainty I ask myself, "Why would my Father asked me such a question?" My thoughts then continued on the word "now." Now is now; nothing to gain and nothing to loose, it is just "now." He then went on to say, *Tangela you spend much of your time in your past crying over the mistakes, hurts, and pains you have endured throughout your life. Then you realize you are no longer there, but the strong grasps of yesterday's hands haven't ceased their sturdy grips or strongholds on you. You quickly jump into the future and begin quoting scriptures of prosperity, success, healing, and blessings like they have taught you to do in church. Hoping some how that this would erase all of the negative thinking you just did and maybe even take some, if not all, of the pain away.*

GOD again asked me, "*What is now? You are missing out on the life I have given you. Your children long for your presence in their life. They need and want your opinion about everything they say and do, whether they want to admit it or not. Your daughter is growing into a beautiful young woman. She will need your help on how to develop into a whole person lacking nothing in spirit, mind and soul. She is in need of your assistance to gradually disclose the hidden treasures that I have placed inside of her and your sons. They need to know their mother has their back no matter what might happen to them in life. A daughter learns how to care for her husband by watching her mother. She watches her mother in everyday task; day in and day out. She watches and listens to what she says and her actions she has toward her husband and family.* (Remember your actions speak louder than your words could ever speak.) *Your daughter observes your attitude very attentively while you're being a helpmate to your husband and family. The attitude she will have about marriage and children will come from the everyday routine of* **your** *life. Have you asked yourself lately what your actions are saying to your children about how you feel towards them and marriage? Your sons were and are still watching their father taking note of how he treats you as a woman and a wife. They listen to how their father speaks and gives respect to women. They see the good or bad behavior their father practices in front of them. By watching and listening to him, this is training for your sons to learn how to choose and communicate with their wives. Your sons are learning what to say to them and what not to say. He's listening how to say the words that would create an environment of peace, joy and love making in the home. Are they hearing words that would send any man, young or old, looking for a roof top to climb onto?* Joyce Myers said it like this, "Words are containers of power." Words have the power to destroy or to give life. We make the choice by what we say to our children, spouses, family members, and friends. God was forcing me to examine my words and actions because I was modeling womanhood for my kids and shaping my future.

Chapter 1

Seeing the results of our words

Back in 1998 God spoke these words to me: *"Words are seeds looking for an open spirit to be planted into. What have you planted into your loved ones today?"* When God spoke this amazing truth to me, I was so ashamed of the words I was speaking to my family. When I was angry, anger came out; when I was bitter, bitterness came spilling out all over everything I loved and held dear to my life. I was destroying the very thing God promised me when I was a little girl growing up in Arizona. One of the places God and I would meet was the clothes line in my mother's back yard. While hanging up the wash, I would freely release my dreams and visions to Him. I was praying the *sun* would not only dry the wet clothes, but somehow the **son** could dry my tears and make all my dreams come true. I wanted to marry a preacher's son who loved God more than he loved me. For some crazy reason I believed I could make it into heaven if I married a preacher's son. God granted me my prayer. I did marry a preacher's son and what a journey it has been. I wanted children so I could give them the love I missed while I was growing up. I had all these things and so much more, but yet I was not happy. God placed everything I prayed for when I was a little child right in my hands. My job was to mold and shape his gifts to me according to His word and His will; not my will. But.....I chose to use my words of brokenness to paralyze the truth about what I could be. This only perpetuated the lie that was told to me about who I was. This lie came from my grandparents who told my parents who and what they could be. Remember, in order for a lie to be passed down from one generation to the next, their must be some facts at the root of the lie. But the facts of the circumstances or words about me are not always the *truth*.

words are seeds

God said this to me, *"Words are spiritual paint brushes, painting on the canvas of our lives. They paint the power of our imagination bringing forth images that lay dormant or hidden until God whispers."* A whisper from God is simply His breath releasing life giving words into our lives to recreate what the Father has already spoken. Each breath of God brings about a new connotation in itself. The word connotation means to suggest or imply in addition to literal meaning. We must understand that a *word* is not just a *word*. A word is the doorway to many meanings of life. Words are only the outer wrapping or packaging on how we feel about our life and the world around us. Words were created to describe life and emotions that we feel. They also allow us to communicate with humanity and all of God's creations.

A word holds within itself the ability to recreate our imagination. When linked with other words and understanding, we have the potential to establish new life and transform those around us. All of this is done by simply releasing our words. Proverbs 18:21 states this truth about the words we speak to ourselves and other people; *"Death and life are in the power of the tongue and they who indulge in it shall eat the fruit of it [for death or life]."* Yes our words are our beginnings of life or death. We choose their destiny in the content of each spoken word we release. A word is a sound released into our mind that produces an understanding into our conscienceness. That understanding is then transmitted to our members to respond or react. An example of this would be someone calling out my name in a foreign or unknown language I didn't understand. I could hear the words (sound) but my mouth or my members would not respond to the person calling me. My understanding could not recognize the words (sound) the person was saying to me. It is very important for us to understand and recognize the principles of a word (sound). This is how we communicate when we speak.

When we understand our words, it changes how we speak and respond to our loved ones, co-workers, and the person on the street. This understanding of our words will help us become better acquainted with our inner voice that speaks to us all the time. This inner voice is telling us the positive and the negative qualities of our character. It is in this dialogue with ourselves and others that our words will determine whether we are successful or a failure in this life. But remember failure is not final, it can be a doorway to change. The inner voice and the words we speak to ourselves and others are the beginning and the ending of the spiritual battle within all of us. It starts with us and ends with us. We must find that place where the Spirit of God dwells or we may never find our way back to "now." Our words play a key role in creating that atmosphere where the spirit of God keeps us in the now.

Chapter 2

Words are the Spiritual paint brushes of life

Before a word becomes a sound that we can release into the atmosphere, God has already created a spirit that is attached to that word (sound). For an example: If you are a positive person, you will speak positive words to your self and those around you. You will have people coming up to you saying, "I was having a bad day until I talked to you" or, "After talking to you, I might have to reconsider the divorce." Every word has a designated spirit or energy connected to it. We must be careful what we release into the atmosphere. Words are the spiritual paint brushes of God that we release into our lives and the people around us.

Words paint in agreement with the views and wishes of ourselves and others to achieve some form of reality we want to see manifested. The spirit that is released from a word has an assignment to bring about what God has ordained and established in the earth. Or the spirit can bring forth what you are saying that is different from His word. The choice is yours each time you speak a word. Will your words be full of faith to bring about what God has already said about the situation? Or will your words be full of feelings and emotions that are contrary to His words? Remember, the spirit and the word becomes one and the same when spoken, and there is nothing greater than the power of agreement. When you hear the word (sound), the spirit enlightens your understanding and floods your imagination with energy to create what you have heard. The words we choose to release have the ability to change and rebuild the atmosphere in any of our situations. They will bring about just what we have spoken into that concern. Yes, *one* word goes far past its literal meaning to bring forth the original *connotation* God created it to be. Please keep in mind that God is the creator of words, spirits, and sounds. He is the one who gave us languages and the capability to use and understand them.

The word connotation also means *to involve as a condition or consequence.* The word involve simply means *to complicate, twist, confuse, tangle or to complex.* This is what **SIN** has done to the human language when we allowed the devil to become involved in the lives of *mankind* back in the Garden of Eden. The confusion of who we are has distorted our imagination and has caused us to have an identity crisis about our origin in God. This identity crisis leaves us with a break in our communication with each other and God. We carry within our spirits twisted images full of misunderstanding that further distorts the truth about us. The consequence of this gross involvement of sin has left mankind in a condition of brokenness. It also leaves us bewildered in understanding the depth and height of the love God has for us. Our words then lack the love of God in each paint stroke we speak onto our spiritual canvas. Our self-hood is unclear, leaving us with expressions of low self-esteem, self-hatred, and jealousy. Our self-centeredness and individuality is no longer centered in the word of God. This leaves us with painted pictures of disfigurement and discontent from our words.

The words that we choose to believe or give our faith to can leave some people in a gender identity crisis. Our inner dialogue continues to defile and pollute man's spirit causing a bigger rift between man and his creator. When each of our words begins to paint on our canvas, the picture becomes unclear because of the lack of communion with our heavenly father. The picture can only become clear when we exchange His words for our words. Only then will we become what he intended us to be. We must say what God has said to us in our communion with him so he can release the energy needed to change our lives.

allow God's energy to manifest

Let's not forget, God is the energy source spiritually, physically, and eternally of all life forms. God is much more than a spirit He is the energy that continues life. For without God there is no life. So, when God speaks, He releases His power to create what He has imagined in His spirit. God is a releaser of energy. He is existence. He is thought. When we pray, we should exchange our energy. This is when we release our words for God's renewing power. Prayer is an exchange of words (energy) that causes a transformation to take place. This transformation takes place in man's spirit first and then in his body. God's word is the energy force transcending through all forms. This is why we can lay hands on the sick, blind, or any other situation and release God's energy to recreate what He has already spoken. Prayer is all about speaking back to God what He has said, declared, and established. This is what Jesus was doing in the Bible. He was just speaking and manifesting what the Father had already spoken. Jesus knew the will of His Father and had no problem repeating the word back to Him. Jesus didn't come to change the word of God. He came to speak it and allow God's energy to manifest what was ordained by God in the beginning. Only when we make the same choices Jesus did and say what God said about us from the beginning of time, can we become what he intended for us to *be* in the present.

Our words will also articulate and orchestrate the movement of our lives. What does **movement** mean? Movement means *to follow some specified course; to change posture or position; to stir the emotions; to turn according to a prescribed motion.* This is how our words direct our path in life. Motion means *the action or process of change of position; the ability or power to move; a prompting from within.* This is how the hand of the *Holy Spirit* encourages us to change and move into a position that God has created just for us. This impulse or inclination about the purpose of God in our life has the power to break strongholds and depression off our minds. If we would only choose to let His presence encompass our entire being (spirit, body, and soul) then we would be able to see our now more clearly.

Words have a way of telling on us. Words connect images to the most secretive areas of our lives. Then our mouths dare to invite other people around us into our hidden world of silence by verbalizing what the inner man of our soul is feeling. This verbalization from our words releases imagery of self expressions into the hearers mind. This leaves the receiver of our words with a mere glimpse of our intellect. It also gives the receiver of our expressions a mere glimpse of our intellect. Words are like keys to the mind; they unlock and enhance the mysteries of the world to the intellect. Our mental power is an untapped potential that lies dormant, undeveloped and sleeping until one word or a statement from God causes man's spirit to experience a lifetime of change.

words can become new life

Remember, it was God's words that moved across the face of the earth to bring forth life out of that which was *void* and *empty*. The Amplified Bible says this in Proverbs 23:7 at the beginning of the verse: "*For as he thinks in his heart, so is he.*" Meaning the power that is produced in the imagination of the mind and is acted upon can become only an outward shell of that man. IF what he is thinking is *not* lining up with what God has already spoken over his life, that man is violating the very purpose of his own existence. Words can become new life or final judgments, depending on the person or persons who are speaking over your life *and* you choose to receive their words. Failure is **only** the inability to accomplish God's purpose. However, what most people think is failure is a judgment of words that we conceive in our spirit as the *truth*. Therefore, we then speak what we believe. Our ineffectiveness to achieve the game of life starts when one's imagination no longer produces words that give life. It too becomes like the face of the earth in the beginning, void and empty waiting for the breath of God to speak again into the emptiness of our minds. Our words can also be the breath of life, like God, if we choose to speak and think the same as He does. It's all a matter of what we choose to speak.

Words can only reproduce the images that are assigned to them. When one speaks the names of their spouses, children, or a dear friend, the image of that person appears alone with the emotions they have towards those people. Words not only have assigned images, but they also have assigned feelings that stir up man's spirit and cause the atmosphere in his inner self to be altered. Yes, words can alter the spirit of man. All of this is done by a simple word that has the *power to change us,* or a group of words that can change the atmosphere of one person or a group. In Isaiah 41:4 God speaks these words, "*Who hath wrought and done it, calling the generations from the beginning? I the LORD, the first, and with the last; I am he.*" It really is all about Him. It is God's continuous uninterrupted **words** that have brought forth the generations from the beginning and His word alone continues to bring us forth. With each generation comes new purpose and understanding of who He is.

Our self expression is so very important to God that He gave us several ways to express our love and gratitude towards Him. We were created to give Him a *willing* praise from our hearts, mind, and soul. We should echo His goodness and mercy throughout time by telling the world *who* God is through the words and images we have experienced God in. When God explained to me why He created the *seed* that would produce generations, it blew my mind because of the simplicity of God. What does God mean by the *seed* that would produce generations?

Chapter 3

God is looking for a particular image of himself

Before man had a spirit or a body, God had a **THOUGHT** about man. He said, *"I need a perpetual praise of my achievements on the earth."* In other words, God was saying to me that He needed a praise that would start in eternity and last indefinitely. He wants to prolong His very own existence in man so He too could be remembered. God has asked the question just like man has asked himself for centuries, "Would it have ever mattered if I existed?" Man has always struggled with his own mortality but where do you think he got it from? The origin of this thought from God didn't come from a place where there was no self identity, for God created.....so therefore He saw his own self expressions in all he created. But it came from a place of self love. God simply wanted to give and receive love from himself. This is the simplest explanation why man was created. Psalms 145: 1-4 said this about man praising God, *"I will extol thee, my*

CHAPTER THREE

God, O King; and I will bless thy name for ever and ever. Every day will I bless thee; and I will praise the name for ever and ever. Great is the Lord, and greatly to be praised; and his greatness is unreachable. One generation shall praise thy works to another, and shall declare thy mighty acts." Our sole purpose is to praise God in the earth.

The heart (spirit) and mind (emotions) of man are connected by using words to verbalize what they are feeling. The spirit of man was also created to praise the Father. God created inside us self-expressions that would bypass mere words and allow our spirit to speak directly to him. Our Father knew not only our mind and heart needed a voice, but the spirit needed one too. In Romans 8:26 the Living Bible makes this point clear, *"And in the same way by our faith the Holy Spirit helps us with our daily problems and in our praying. For we don't even know what we should pray for, not how to pray as we should; but the Holy Spirit prays for us with such feeling that it cannot be expressed in words."* To silence man's spirit means to die a spiritual death. Remember people who are paralyzed, deaf, blind, and mute still have the ability to express their spirit. The spirit is different from the soul (mind, will, and emotions) and it too must be heard. All these elements paint the final picture of our life-time that will be judged by God who is the author and the finisher of our faith.

Words come from the depth of man's spirit, reproducing what his beliefs are. They can come from places we have experienced or emotional rooms we have lived in for years. These are just two containers where one can store up their faith or their disbelief while walking through this journey called life. Remember, words are our self-expressions. Words can paint pictures of our life and leave them hanging in rooms of our past. It then becomes our choice to leave them there in the past or pack them up and take them with us on our way to our next active participation in life. The final canvas is only finished when the last word is spoken over your life. Then the creator judges the canvas. He alone knows how the painting should look. God knows the right amount of intensity needed to create the impression that should be left on the canvas after each *hair* of the paint brush is stroked in its proper place. Each stroke is filled with enough passion to complete the finished work God had in mind. God is looking for a particular image of himself before he makes His judgment.

we see the results of what we have spoken

God takes into consideration all aspects of our lives before making His final judgment. The whys, what for, and the many other excuses we use when we are missing some master strokes. He would ask us, "*What happened to the greatness I gave you in this area of your life? What did you do with it? There are strokes of kindness missing when I sent you people to show them my love. I gave you my imagination and my word full of power so you could imagine what I would do and say in any of your situations. But yet, the picture is not complete in this area; why? I see some strokes that shouldn't be here like anger, strife, unforgiveness and low self-esteem. You took my word, but you refused to apply it to this area of your life. Why? The powerful force of your rejection isolated you from your spouse, children, friends and even me. I sent these people as your support group and yet you rejected them too. You prayed for my help day and night. But because it didn't come the way you expected, say the things you needed to hear, and look the way you wanted it to look, you rejected me as well as my help.*" Until you are ready to recognize the hand of God in others, God cannot help you. We must take a very long and hard look at our life and ask this question: Is my life a portrait of what God intended it to be or is it a series of one bad portrait after another? Remember the paint brush is in your hand so stop blaming other people for the portrait of your life.

Let's not get angry at God's judgments because His judgments are just and true. The anger must start with us and end there too. The painting is only a representation of our words in action. We speak and therefore we see the result of what we have spoken over our own lives. Yet, we get angry about the paint strokes we have painted onto our canvas. As if someone else came by, took the brush out of your hand and started painting lies about you while God did nothing but allow them to do so. Life is full of people who want to hurt us and do us no good at all, but we must not permit the bloody strokes of life to harm the perfect portrait of **truth** that lies just beneath our surface. Do we really know the truth about ourselves?

it is the Lord's doing.....

One day, as I was stepping out of my shower, God told me to go stand in front of the bathroom mirror. I stood there in all of my glory, only wearing the skin that He provided for me at birth. He went on to say these words to me, "This is the Lord's doing and it's marvelous in His sight" (Psalm 118:23). I dropped my head and one tear ran down my cheek. He told me to hold my head up and He then repeated himself again, "It is the Lord doing and it's marvelous in His sight." My negative words met my lips before I knew it. But God would not let me speak them. God kept on saying it over and over again. I looked at myself in that same mirror to try to see what my Father was seeing. I saw a fat, overweight person who had nothing but scars from her past trying to defeat her. This person I saw believed in her heart that absence from the body means presence with the Lord. If it were to happen today, it couldn't come soon enough. He then told me to repeat it out loud so I could hear His words coming out of my mouth and bring truth to my ears. The tears flowed and I received a spiritual cleaning like no other. It was far better than any bath or shower I could ever get here on earth. I could feel the hands of the Holy Spirit washing away some of my low self-image. Water alone couldn't remove the hardness and the poison lying beneath my layer of skin. If my Father could love me in this state of impureness of low self-esteem, then my Father must really love me for who I am and not what my words are saying about myself.

Our words are a silent language that converse with the inner man of our soul. Words carry within itself the secrets places of God. It is our spirit wrapped within our words that allow us to enter into the throne room of God to plead our case or to bless His holy name. Remember, no flesh will have glory in His presence, so we must send our words before us proclaiming His goodness in order to enter in. When one gets the *right* understanding of a word, it is like opening the window just in time to see God's hinder parts walking by. In Proverbs 9:10 it says this, *"The fear of the Lord is the beginning of wisdom: and the knowledge of the holy is understanding."* In this passage the word *fear* means: to be in awe or to give an individual who is in an exalted position reverence and render him proper respect. The word *fear* also implies submission; to submit yourself under God's wisdom, knowledge and understanding to better appreciate Him and His word.

Knowledge, in it's simplest form is the understanding of words that is followed by man's corresponding actions. A Godly action cannot happen until understanding of God's word is conceived. Conception will give birth to what was copulated between the words understood by man and his actions. To copulate is *to fasten together or link*. An example of this happens when we tell our children to go clean their rooms. Parents explain to them what we want done and then we ask them if they understand. The child usually nods and off they go to their room to complete the task. The child returns in about a half hour and says, "I'm finished cleaning my room." The parent goes into the child's room and almost everything you told the child to do is not done. Why? The words you spoke to the child did not reproduce the right action because there was no true understanding of your words. With take this same knowledge and this is how we treat our heavenly Father and His word. We *say* we understand Him and the words he speaks to us daily, but our actions towards others do not portray what we say we know. I kept finding myself stuck in a wilderness of knowing His words, but I was not applying them to my life. If I had applied the word to my life, then a lasting change could have taken place and lead to Godly actions. God can and will determine our knowledge of Him and our understanding of His word based on our actions.

no true intimacy

Dr. Myles Munroe is one of my spiritual fathers in Christ. His book entitled "Understanding the purpose and power of PRAYER" is a must read. He makes this statement on page 152 of his book, *"Mental assent looks so much like faith that many people cannot see the difference between the two. Mental assent means intellectually accepting the Word as true-admiring it and agreeing with it-but not allowing it to have an impact on you, so that it doesn't do you any good. In essence, mental assent agrees with God but does not believe God."* In reading his chapter, I had to put down the book and repent. I knew God but I did not want to allow Him to be intimate with me. I accepted His word but there were things I was not **doing**. I agreed with the word of God, but there were so many things in my life that I agreed with God about but I did not really believe Him. There was no true intimacy.

I was in a relationship with God but I did not want it to be intimate. This is like saying you are married to your husband for many years, but never had sexual intercourse with him because you didn't want to get too close and intimate with him. The bible tells us we are to be doers not just hearers of His word (James 1:23). Ladies, sex is a part of marriage. If you say you are married, then the act of love making should be a part of it. We show our husbands we love them when we perform this intimate act of lovemaking frequently. This is our actions replacing our words. Just as with God, I knew what I was supposed to do and would be faithful executing His word in my life...... for a while. Until life came in and overwhelmed me to the point I too said, "What is the point in praying? If God wants this to happen, it will. All the praying in the world can't change the mind of God on this matter." I then treated God like I treated my husband when he wouldn't listen to me. I simply ignored God and all His needs. (Yes our Father has needs too.) I was a person who had given up on herself and the word of God. Until one

17

day when I asked God to show Himself to me. I told God, "If you are really God and you stand by your word, then show me you." Boy did He show himself to me. I became intimate with God and His word when His Holy Spirit impregnated me with God's understanding of His word.

Understanding of words is the fruit that comes from knowledge. Knowledge misunderstood is power misused. This understanding should be implemented into our everyday life, not just when we think we may need help from God. The power that comes from understanding a *single* word can change your entire life. Every word you will ever read in your life will always ask this one question, "**How deep do you want to go in understanding all aspects of me?**" Remember, one simple word can have many meaning........so which meaning of the word will liberate your spirit? The deeper you dig, the more it will release its true nature (riches) called *illumination*. These are some of the things I had to come to grips with when God showed me my missing parts from my canvas and a tear ran down my face as if there was no more time to *change*. I realized I was destroying my family with the words I was choosing to say to them and it needed to stop **NOW**! The Way Living Bible in Proverbs 11:29 puts it in these words, *"The fool who provokes his family to anger and resentment will finally have nothing worthwhile left."* The Good New Bible in Proverbs 11:30 also states, *"Righteousness gives life, but violence takes it away."* A good example of a destructive word is the word divorce. Remember, the beginning of a divorce starts with a thought (seed) that comes from a negative word that was spoken out aloud. It all starts with the thought or seed of what we think of marriage.

where are your sons?????

What most men are looking for in a wife but won't admit, is an updated version of all the *good qualities* they have found in their mother. Mothers are the first and lasting impression of intimacy with a woman. This lasting impression will stay with the man until he finds a wife or truly falls in love. Their wife can only be compared to what the man has experienced throughout his childhood. They long to be nurtured and edified from the loving breasts of their wives who exhibit their mother's good characteristics. God then asked me, "*Where are your male children that I have given to you?*" The reason why my father asked me this question was because my oldest son and I didn't have a good relationship. I stopped trying to have one with him. I found it was too painful to open up to another male in my life and take a chance that he may reject me also. When my oldest son was entering into his teenage years, he was finding it very hard to fit in at school, church, and home. I wanted to keep the son who was obedient, trustworthy, and full of fun. He was the one who could make the whole family laugh. My oldest son was the only one who would watch alien movies with me anytime, day or night. But I was slowly losing touch with him.

I saw him rebelling and drifting away from my husband and I. His grades in school kept getting lower and lower. My husband and I tried everything. We would go to the school and talk with his teachers. His father would spend long hours helping him with his homework. But the lies kept coming and grades kept getting lower and lower. My depression started growing and became even more painful. I felt it was entirely my fault because I some how failed him as a mother. My husband and I both wanted to know what more we could do to help him transition through adolescent to teen years. God had the answer waiting for me but I refused to do it because I thought it would be a waste of my time and tears.

God wanted me to tell my son about my adolescence years and how I struggled with rebellion and fitting in. But my response to God's request was no. He is my son and not someone I needed to answer to. I don't have to explain myself to him or anyone in my household. I am the parent and he is the child, (ever heard that before). I do not have to tell him about the many mistakes I made while raising him. How could a child who was trying to understand being a teenager, understand adult problems and issues? These and many other thoughts ran through my mind while my Father asked me repeatedly to talk to my son. My son needed me to talk to him and restore his confidence. He needed me to let him know the family unit would stay together no matter what was going on in the home. He needed me to say to him, "*What you are going through is only a part of life to get you to adulthood. So please don't take your anger out on yourself or your family. We are the people who love you.*" But I couldn't put words to my pain back then, so I left him to figure out things on his own. Son, mom is so very sorry for not being there for you while you were trying to grow into manhood. Please forgive me for my carelessness on how I handled you and the situation.

I had a lot to learn about life

God responded to me with this, "*Yes, you may know where your sons are physically, but spiritually they are far from you. Your oldest son, you pushed him away because of the pressures of being a young mother and not married. Yes, you felt the shame and embarrassment each time you and your son went around your family. While he was growing up into manhood, you had nothing good to say to him. You were more concerned with training and teaching him how to behave in public instead of getting your own issues resolved with your own father. Your issues with your own father have impacted the way you have treated your sons, husband and the men in your life.*" I knew it was the voice of God but I ignored Him anyway.

Yes, it was my oldest son who gave me back a reason to live again. The road to destruction had my name written all over it, and the welcoming arm of hell was waiting at the end of it. I was on my way to drugs, men, and partying all the time during my freshman year at Arizona State University. I thought I had fallen in love with a sophomore who was on the wrestling team. I was young, inexperienced and a virgin. I had a lot to learn about life and for some crazy reason, I was in a big hurry to learn as much as possible at a very young age. But the hand of God was all over my life even back then. Getting pregnant my freshmen year of college changed everything for me. That is why I believe my son was and still is my angel of rescue. Why? Because now I had this small child and it wasn't all about me anymore.

I would sit wondering what to do with this small child of mine. I kept saying to myself, I must be taking care of one of my mother's children. My mother had eleven children and all of us were living in one small house together. I am the sixth child and I had 5 older sisters and brothers. I also had five younger siblings and it was the job of my sister, Vyinne, and I to bathe, feed, clothe and look after the younger ones. In the back of my mind, I kept saying, "One day my mom will want this child back because this child can't be mine. But in the meantime, my mind was flooded with questions. Who will help me with this child? Where will the finances come from to feed, to shelter, and to clothe this child? Yes, I was willing to work and work hard to try to make all of his dreams come true, but what if I can't do it? Will he too grow up and hate me like I hated my parents? The doubts, worries and shame of having a child out of wedlock kept me trying to prove to myself and to my mother that I was a good mother. But there lies part of my problem.

My mother rarely cheered me on. I kept my son spotless and his clothes were always tight and on point. I moved in with one of my sisters but I still kept my son neat and clean. When you saw me, you saw my child and we were one. If a man was going to love me, then he had to love my son also. You couldn't have me without respecting and loving my son too. But the problem was still there. Even now I long to hear those words coming out of my mother's mouth to confirm me as a person, a mother, and a wife. It would be like getting that Christmas present I always wanted as a child. But my mother couldn't give to me what she hadn't received as a child.

You reproduce what you are

y spiritual father, Apostle Sammy C. Smith, who is also a pastor, said the most awesome words that I now see the results of in my children and in my life today. He said, *"You can teach what you know, but you reproduce what you are."* Teaching is the transferring of knowledge and information verbally through ones words or actions. The reproduction of oneself is a spiritual principle that God set in order in the beginning of time. It is called the transferring of spirits or generational curses or blessings. Blessings and curses come from the words that have been spoken over a person and then believed as the truth (Deuteronomy chapters 27 and 28). We have a choice to act like our parents or those who live in our personal environment. Our choice of which we become will be based on the spirit or the words we submit ourselves to. So what spirit are you speaking over your kids to submit to? I was submitting myself to the words my mother had spoken over me.

Parents, please keep this in mind about your children. *Children are a heritage of the Lord; and the fruit of the womb is his reward. As arrows are in the hand of a mighty man; so are children of your youth (Psalms 127:3-4 King James.)* Children may be the arrows that come from our bodies, but God has given parents the assignment of launching them into life and releasing them into *their* destiny. Not into what **you** think they should be, but into what God has called them to be. Knowing your child's destiny is just as important to God as providing and caring for them. He has given every parent the tools to seek out purpose for every seed that He has allowed to come forth out of the woman's womb. But God also gave the man a very important role in this process.

it will take God to complete you

Bishop Eddie Long made this powerful statement that confirms why God made the man the head of woman. He said this, "*Man was created to protect and <u>provide for what comes out of woman</u>.*" Why? Because man gave birth to a woman, not a child. God created man, not woman, to bring forth a fully grown woman. She was whole in spirit, body and soul. She was lacking nothing from a man or a woman. Yes, her frame was birthed out of man's body only once. But her intellect, awareness, and consciousness came from the spirit of God. She didn't go looking for another man's (father) or woman's (mother) approval for what she was to be. It was not man's sperm or woman's womb that created the first woman. She was complete by the hands of God and God only. God alone completed her. It was God that completed the first woman and it will take God to complete you, not a man. Man's job is to protect and to provide for what God has already put inside the WO-MAN or a man with a womb. The womb that is inside of a WO-MAN has many hidden treasures waiting to be discovered.

Adam's job is to discover and cultivate the seeds inside of a woman so they will produce the Godly fruit the Father intended. But the things inside of a woman came from God and not man. Eve was complete with destiny and purpose *before* God presented her to Adam. There was **no** co-dependence between Adam and Eve. They didn't need one to complete the other. Adam was clueless in the sight of God pertaining to the help he would need to subdue and have dominion over the earth. Remember, WO-MAN was God's idea, not man's. God didn't consult Adam about any aspect of WO-MAN or the help she would provide for him and mankind.

When woman opened her eyes, she saw her existence and the Father of creation. God alone spoke to her about purpose, helpmate, and the birthing of those things which are spiritual visions and dreams. God and woman walked and talked together as Father and daughter. She was smitten by His glory and captivated by His love. God was the *first* and last object of her desire. I can imagine the Father showing her the wonder of Himself that was found deep inside of her. Saying, "*Daughter, you too have this same likeness to recreate life spiritually as well as physically. Yes, life also flows from your belly to the earth.*" They communed together and time was not a factor. Our Father did not want to rush this vital step in the making of WO-MAN. She would be the help man needed. Adam was sleeping and knew nothing about the precious and priceless gift of love that God was preparing for him. And then the Father of creations presented her to Adam who named her Eve. Naming Eve was the **only** step that God gave him the authority to do in the *finishing* of woman.

In this finishing step of creating and releasing WO-MAN, she needed a name. God gave the responsibility of naming her to the male called Adam. Telling him, *"Adam what you name, you claim **responsibility** for."* Adam understood the responsibility of naming because he was naming the animals. He also understood the role of leadership he had to assume in naming them. Adam's position of accountability holds a very powerful task to him or the persons who dares to assume its authority. Responsibility is defined in Webster's dictionary as: *liable to be called on to answer; liable to be called to account as the primary cause, motive, or agent; able to answer for one's conduct and obligations; trustworthy; able to choose for oneself between right and wrong.* Remember ladies, God didn't give Adam the ability to make or create WOMAN, he gave him the ability to name and define WO-MAN.

To define something or someone simply means having the ability to **name** and to give identity to. Adam, the male, was willing to name and to give his identity, the spirit of man, to Eve, the fe-male. In giving Eve her name, Adam was releasing what God already placed inside of woman. In fact, Adam recognized **him-self** in her. In Adam the *male,* he saw Eve. Adam saw individuality, uniqueness, distinctiveness, and **self** all in the female. All Adam did was come into agreement with what God wanted to be released in woman. Adam began to speak God's words over WO-MAN and she became what Adam declared and decreed according to the word. Adam named Eve, therefore, God gave him the responsibility of caring for her and their offspring. None of this happened until after God the father was finished creating and molding woman. Then the father presented her to Adam.

knowing your position.....

God did **not** present her to Adam before God explained to her what her purpose was to Him, first, and then to man. Ladies, lets not get them out of order; God first and then man. Which one did we see first? Was it God or the man? Remember, our God is a jealous God. In Dueteronomy 4:2, the Bible states, *For the Lord thy God is a consuming fire, even a jealous God.* God wants to be the first one to make love to you with His words. He wants you to serve Him first to set your life in order. He wants us to love and serve man but not before we love and serve God. Ladies, **let's not get God and man out of position**. When we misplace their order, we too get caught up in the misplacement of which one we will serve first. Then we find ourselves out of position with God.

God at no time has ever taken a side from a woman and then molded and fashioned that side into a fully grown man. God did not ask a woman what she would like to name man. We as women must not get out of our established position. Our position is a **set** place that God has created for woman. When a woman understands her position, she understands her power. The word *position* has two implied meanings. The first is *poise*. It is a particular posture of carrying oneself when understanding destiny. Poise means to balance. Women are the balancer of man. We are the life givers. We hold and carry the equilibrium of man and mankind. *Equilibrium* in this statement simply means the intellectual or the emotional balance that is needed to continue humanity. The second part of the word *position* implies the meaning to sit. *To sit* means to have ones dwelling place. To dwell; to be in a highly favorable situation; to maintain one's position without change. When you put the two meanings together, you come up with a woman of balance who positions herself in a highly favorable situation with knowledge of her purpose in God. It's vital for man and woman to understand their position and *dwell* in it.

the first line of defense for the woman

Remember back in Genesis when Eve ate the forbidden fruit, sin was conceived in her. But the fall of man did not happen until Adam's actions were disobedient to God. Men are essential parts that makeup mankind. To take away a man out of any relationship will be detrimental to the family and to society. The removal of man would destroy the social order that God has ordained and established. The men would suffer, but the women and children will feel an even greater loss. To take the man out of the family is like taking out the governing power. You take out all of its laws and precepts leaving only a shell of society to work with. Who then would defend man's inner parts that God removed from his side? This is why it will **always** be so very important to have a man's presence in the lives of our children. In staying in our "now" we must comprehend and respect the positioning of God in mankind. Yes, it takes a man to make a man, and it takes a man to make a WO-MAN.

Man gave birth to a fully grown mature woman without the pain of labor or travailing. With the help of God's hands and no understanding of sin at that time, woman was brought forth from man's side. Therefore the responsibility of giving birth to humanity lies in man's hand to protect. Man was and still is woman's covering. God created man and put woman inside of him. Woman was waiting for God's appointed time for man to release woman and her seeds that are found in her life giving womb. This is one of the reasons why man is responsible or is called "The head of the family." Man's job is to be a *protector* of any relationship between man, woman, and their offspring. The definition for being a protector or to protect is *to be a cover or a shield from exposure, injury or destruction.* We are reminded in the Bible that the devil comes to kill, steal, and destroy humanity at all cost. Man should be the first line of defense for the woman and her offspring. This is where the father, brother, pastor, or any male in her life should assume this role. Protect means to maintain the status of integrity through financial or legal guarantees. Yes, in the traditional roles, the man should work and work smarter. He should not work harder than his parents to provide for his family by learning from their experiences. The word protect also implies, supervision or support of one that is smaller and weaker.

In 1 Peter 3:7 the bible makes this statement about the woman being the weaker vessel, *"Likewise, ye husbands, dwell with them according to knowledge, giving honour unto the wife, as unto the weaker vessel, and as being heirs together of the grace of life: that your prayers be not hindered."* Man being the head must provide supervision for his family. Let's break up the word *super-vision.* The first part of that word means; *over and above the norm that is found in most people.* The second word is *vision;* which is *unusual discernment or foresight; the act or power of seeing.* Put the two together and you have *supervision, a critical watching and directing of activities or a course of action.* It is man's job to come up with **a plan for life** along with the helpmate God has provided for him. He must ensure the vision God has for the family will manifest clearly. Man is to take care of the *sum* balance of God's creation. The **sum** means the amount obtained as a result of God adding to his rib. He is the counterbalance. He is a force or an influence between creation and humanity. But God connected all of mankind by placing the spirit of Adam in women so they can work together with man.

know the destiny of every seed

It is the spirit of Adam that dwells inside of woman's body that helps us to stay stable and focus. The spirit of Adam is likened to the rudder of a ship at sea. When a child is born, God launches the baby into the world equipped with everything to bring that child back to the Father. The rudder represents the second Adam (Jesus) that can lead man and woman back to God if they choose to return to Him. The family was birthed out of the man called Adam and all of the seeds God brought forth from him. All of mankind, men, women, and children, were birthed out of Adam, including Eve. The seeds from Adam were planted inside Eve by God. Men, or the male must continue to plant seeds inside of women, or the female man. She then nurtures those seeds and gives birth. Every seed inside a woman, from God and man, will be matured and birthed. That is why it is so very important to know the destiny of every seed that comes forth out of woman. You must know the origin and destiny of every seed. Children represent God's inheritance and he gave parents the responsibility of helping each seed reach it's destiny. This is truly being a godly parent watching over His inheritance. But this is where you have to stay in the "Now" for you and your seeds.

This is where I lost the power of **now** so many times because I didn't know the male role in my life. I believed if you wanted something in this life, you fight for it tooth and nail. Even if you are fighting with the person who is supposed to be helping you get to your destiny. My motto in life was, "*If you don't take care of you, no one else will.*" I had tried Jesus and I felt like He let me down too. So why would I trust anyone in my life **NOW**? It was that continuous choice I repeatedly made that left me in my past mistakes. I had to relive those choices over and over again until the sprit of life left me. It left me with the spirit of suicide because I saw no ending to my past life of pain. I was moving on in life but I was living in the past and the pain was real.

It was a year and a half later that I meet and married my husband. Life then became very interesting for me for many years to come. My husband on the one hand told me I was a great mother and wife. He called me a woman of God and a friend to the friendless. He was so proud to call me his wife. I believed I could do anything on those days. Love making was about praising God and singing out my husband's name. Depression was as far from me as the earth is from the sun. It was during those days that my malnourished spirit desperately clung to. It was me hoping to live in a moment that I knew would never last. It was like having a spiritual orgasm that I would hold on to long after it had dissipated. It would leave me empty with only a memory of what life could be. I lived for my husband's praises and his words created my world. I believed I was good if he said I was and I believed him if he said I wasn't. But there was the problem in me.

Chapter 5

Humpty Dumpty and I

I was lacking self-esteem, value, and purpose. I had no knowledge and understanding of who I was in God. I looked for my husband, my father, my mother, and even my pastor or any headship to define my purpose, position and value in life. If my husband's first wife (United States Air Force) treated him wrong in anyway, or the church didn't fulfill a spiritual need, I would hear about it. Then my mental pedestal that I allowed myself to be placed upon would come crashing down and great was the fall. Humpty Dumpty and I had so much in common.

Humpty Dumpty and I both allowed ourselves to be placed in vulnerable positions. We then depended on other people to come help put us back together again. We both played and starred in the **victim** role. Will someone please come help me, because I refuse to take responsibility for my own life? Humpty and I didn't have to sit on that wall. It was a *choice* we made. We had the power to choose not to sit there, but yet we did. Why did we make such a choice? We made the choice to sit on the wall of life because of the pay off we were getting from sitting on that wall. It would give us the attention we desperately needed in life from our families, friends, and the church. Why else would we choose this wall out in the open for all to see? We wanted to be seen and heard. We knew that all the King's horses and all the King's men would come to our rescue if we fell. Remember, only God can heal the wounded heart (Psalm 147:3). The problem in this situation is that people will gladly put you back together according to *their* own purpose and plans.

it's all about realizing what's inside

I had allowed other people to put my life together but you must know your own purpose and destiny. You must know who you are. If you don't know who you are, there are loved ones, family members, co-workers, and friends that will gladly oblige you with their *own* opinions of who they think you should be. If you don't live up to what they think you should be, you then become disposable to them. You become something they will use and then throw away. You are worthless to them, like the dust in the wind. If that doesn't happen, they might criticize you to a spiritual death, if you choose to listen to them. The key becomes the word of God. Knowing the word of God is like knowing where the true mirror is in your life and asking the difficult questions like: *"Who am I?"*; *"What is my purpose on this earth?"*; or *"Mirror, mirror on the wall, tell me the truth about it all?"* Your life is precious and God's word is the mirror.

It wasn't a coincidence that Humpty Dumpty was an egg. An egg is a fragile but very useful item to have. There is over 101 ways to use an egg. The egg is a very fundamental part in many recipes. Without the egg, the food would fall apart. The chef knows that the egg brings balance and flavor to his recipe. None of this can happen until someone cracks the shell and allows the essential parts of the egg to come out. *It is all about realizing what is inside* the shell. Inside the shell is the necessary flavor and balance that is needed to complete the recipe. The cracking of the shell is all about the *due timing of God*. It takes a master chef to know when, where and how to release the undiluted essential principles for life. Those principles are called God's increase. Inside you are the principles of life and God is the chef.

The problem with Humpty Dumpty and I is we chose to sit on that wall and watch life pass us by. We became stale and rotten, unfit. Then one day Jesus came by and said, *"I am the true vine, and my Father is the husbandman. Every branch in me that beareth not fruit he taketh away; and every branch that beareth fruit, he purgeth it, that it may bring forth more fruit"* (John 15:1-2) If you are sitting on a wall and watching your life go by, don't be surprised when the fall happens. The fall represents **a choice you refused to make**, so God made one for you. If you don't stand for something you will **fall** for anything. What you do after the fall will determine how God will use you for the rest of your life. Once it happens, it is not the fall that kills a man, but it is the **impact** of it.

Only God can put back together the delicate intricate workings of an egg. He and He alone has the blue print of every yoke and its outer shell. God knows how the egg should look from the inside out because even an egg is developed in the womb of His understanding. As Christians or being Christ-like, it is not *if* we fall, *but when we fall*. God has already prepared provision for the **fall of man**. In Psalms 37:23-24 it makes this point very clear, *"The steps of good men are directed by the Lord. He delights in each step they take. If they fall it isn't fatal, for the Lord holds them with his hand"(The Way Bible)*. The main point in the passage is a **good man or woman**. This is one who is trying to do what the Father is saying, but their *issues* seem to have a grip on them. They need help in making the right choices or the changes they need to move forward in life. They are stuck in a cycle or stuck in stupid. They keep repeating the same mistake over and over again. Isn't this the same definition of insanity? Doing the same thing over and over again but expecting a different result? So look at your results and start to examine your choices.

the impact from the fall

A result is only the ending of a beginning choice. The fall is your actions. But the impact from the fall is the results of your spirit being broken. What does it mean to have a broken spirit? Are you remorseful and in need of a change like I was? Please keep on reading. If you want help, it is as close to you as your understanding. *"The Lord is nigh unto them that are of a broken heart; and saveth such as be of a contrite spirit"* (Psalms 34:16). What does the word *contrite* mean? Contrite means **humbled by guilt and repentant for one's sins; broken in spirit; to bruise; contrition: Sincere remorse for wrongdoing; Repentance for sin with a sincere desire**

to amend, arising from pure love of God. The bible also says it this way, *"For a just man falleth seven times, and riseth up again: but the wicked shall fall into mischief"(Proverbs 24:16)*. It will be the fall's impact that will define your life decisions. Will your testimonies from the fall impact the world, or will the fall continue to impact your life? Or will the fall keep you in a cycle of pain? The choice is yours. In other words, each **fall** has a purpose in showing you......you. The fall shows you your choices, the results, and it reveals your flaws.

The fall represents your character flaws. The impact of that fall represents what you do after man has seen your flaws. Do we run and hide behind a fig leaf like Adam did in the Garden of Eden and blame some one else for our mistakes? Or will we go seeking to find the covering of God and allowing Him to *re-present* our life back to Him? Let's stop for just a moment and look a little closer at the word *re-present*. What does that really mean? We say it all the time and read it in many books and papers. What are we really trying to say to one another when we use this word?

Chapter 6

Re-Presenting

The dictionary blew my mind with this simple word, *represent*. It brought a deeper understanding and revelation to a word that is common to me and others. The word *represents* means: *To depict; portray. To present clearly to the mind; To make representations (of something) to someone by way of remonstrance or expostulation; To serve as an example of; produce; show; bring back.* Our lives should show, portray, or serve as an example of the life of Jesus to the world. Our life-*time* is a conglomerate of God bringing us back to a point we would rather not deal with. We say to our father, please help me get past this hurt, pain and emotional stress so I can be healed but by the time God gets us to a point He can deal with the real issues, we take off running in the spirit. Sometimes we take off running in the natural. We make statements of blame like Adam did in the garden. Like Adam, we are not willing to take responsibility for his own actions. These are some of the statements we make today when God *re-presents* our life back to us:

It was somebody else's fault. (Mom, dad, sister, brother, husband or wife)

I didn't mean to hurt them so why should I apologize?

If they had just left me alone, I would not have cussed them out.

I struggle with sex because I was molested.

It was the boss who caused me to get fired.

I know I am overweight but I come from a big boned family.

I could make ends meet if I had more money.

Alcoholism runs in my family so what's the big deal.

If I was (white, black, a man or woman), I would have gotten that promotion.

Why does it seem like I can't make ends meet?

I am not a morning person.

It was because I didn't have a father at home.

My family has always been this way.

I did that because I was abused as a child.

God is continually bringing our choices and words back to us so we can revaluate anything that isn't Christ-like. In bringing our choices, meaning our predetermined actions and words, back to us, God is asking us a question. God asks us, "Would I have said and did the same thing in this situation or circumstance?" If the answer is **no** and in most cases it is, there must be a change in our character and in our way of life. Our heavenly father wants to *re-member* us back together mentally, physically and spiritually. This is why He *re-presents* or brings back our actions and words for us to better understand why we are the way we are. Aren't you tired of seeing the same movie of your life over and over again? Then Change.

stop running from the changes

We must stop running from the changes that are only found in His presence. God presents us with the facts of our life, like He did with Adam, and then gives us an opportunity or a choice to repent. This opportunity to change is called God's grace. Also in James 4:6 it says, "*But He gives us more and more grace (power of the Holy Spirit, to meet this evil tendency and all others fully).* Bishop Eddie Long puts it this way in his tape called "God's Grace." He explained that the grace of God is the time between us committing sin and getting it right with God. It is God giving you a moment to get things correct in His sight. When God told Peter His grace was sufficient in 1 Corinthians 12:9, He was saying the time period that I have given to you is enough for you to stop! Peter asked God three times to please take his thorn in the flesh away from him. But God refused him each time. The thorn was there to remind Peter that it is all about depending on God and not us. We must remind ourselves daily that the power we have comes from

God and at anytime He can take it back without asking our permission. When our Father re-presents our life to us with the facts of us doing wrong in His sight, we must repent. But if we choose not to, like a loving father, He blesses us with another day to get it right; meaning He gives us His Grace. Please keep this in mind; no one knows when God's grace begins and when it will end. So repent and get into His presence so He can help you make the change the next time He *re-presents* your choices to you. Then God can *re-member* you.

We all need God to *re-member* us back together spiritually and emotionally. He is the only one that can go into our yesterdays and make all our facts into the truth about us. He is a mender of broken vessels. Even the sinner at the cross recognized he needed Jesus to *re-member* him when He went to be with the father in heaven. So allow God to re-present your life back to you, until Jesus can re-present Himself (you) to Himself (the Father).

So why does Jesus keep re-presenting our lives to us? In 2 Corinthians 3:2-3 it states this: *"You yourselves are the letter we have, written on our hearts for everyone to know and read. It is clear that Christ himself wrote this letter and sent it by us. It is written, not with ink but with the Spirit of the living God and not on stone tablets but on human hearts."* The same way Jesus walked, talked, and lived on this earth as a man, people should see us and see the life of Him within us. Yes, Jesus was *all* man and *all* God. Jesus had to learn how to activate His anointing while living in the flesh just like we must learn to do the same everyday of our own lives. We must find the NOW of things and live our lives in each minute, moment and instant knowing that "NOW is all we have. The word of God is all we have and all we need to find purpose in our life-time. Tomorrow is not promised to us and neither is the next five minutes. In Isaiah 28:12-13, the Bible talks about how God will show us how to be acquainted with and stay in the NOW of our life. *"He offered rest and comfort to all of you, but you refused to listen to him. That is why the Lord is going to teach you letter by letter, line by line, and lesson by lesson."* Yes, it's true. All we have in this life to help us find our purpose is His word and His Spirit. But God's glory is the moments by moments, seconds by seconds that adds up to this exquisite journey. A journey of all we must pass through and call our life-<u>time</u>.

Every moment and second adds up to our life-time. Please keep this in your mind. It is not the great moves of God that we see in our everyday lives. Our lives are **not** built around the miraculous. Nor do we see two fish and five loafs of bread blessed in front of us to feed five thousand people. Yes, God is teaching us lessons everyday, if we would capture His voice in our *NOW*. We must learn His precepts and guidelines on how to achieve the abundant life that He has promised today. Not yesterday or tomorrow but today. Once the application of His voice has been made in our life, we then can stay in the **power of now** and experience those promises. You must ask yourself this question, "What is God saying to me in this Now?" But staying in the NOW and operating in the power of now is a choice that we must make with every breath we breathe.

Remember, a choice can be an open door for opportunity to expand ones imagination. Dare to dream in the <u>*now*</u> of your life! I was so far from this in my own imagination. I had a form of godliness but I was denying the true power of my heavenly Father in my life. I knew how to dress the part of being saved and I was married to an elder in the church. I knew when to say praise the Lord at the appropriate time in each sermon. I learned how to hide my hurt and pain from my past so I could be used in the church. I wanted to help other bleeding souls like myself who had lost their way too. But my inner conversation of self-hatred, bitterness, and unforgiveness were my friends. We walked together and they talked to me. When they spoke to me, I returned their dialogue. I spoke what self-hatred, bitterness, and unforgiveness told me to say. But our words can be our best friends or our worst enemy. When you saw me, you were also seeing my many friends. We were inseparable and nothing could come between us..........except a *choice*.

a choice

I chose self-hatred, bitterness, and unforgiveness to be my friends and they gladly accepted the invitation to dwell deep inside my spirit as long as my choice was to keep them. They also brought some of their friends to inhabit my mind, body, and soul (anger, verbal abuse and rejection). When my inner friends told me to jump, I quickly said how high? The load of carrying them everywhere I went became burdensome and oppressive. I saw life through their eyes. The picture they were painting was full of self-distortion, deception, and a twisted falsification of the truth about me. I saw nothing through the eyes of Jesus. My spirit cried out for help and Jesus answered me by *re-presenting* my life to me and then asking me to exercise my power of choice to change. One can not hold on tightly to the past and expect something different in tomorrow. Tomorrow will be the same as yesterday until you choose to let go of the past by reaching forward and embracing the impossible of your life. Yes....it is your life's choices that got you here. It will be your life's *choices* that will take you beyond your imagination which will lead you to the throne room of God's presence of **change** for your life. CHOOSE!!

God *re-presents* to us our lives over and over again in every n*ow*, causing us to revaluate our choices. One must always remember all we have is *now*. **Now** is the most imminent place in God. Why? Because **now** is the breath of God in us. If God were to remove His **now** from our lives, we would no longer be here in this existence. In 2 Corinthians 6:16-18 God says, *"I will live in them and walk among them; and I will be their God and they shall be my people. And I will welcome you, and be a Father to you, and you will be my sons and daughters."* You only exist because God allows you to continue to exist. So He should be the first one we please because He gave us this *Now*. If only what we do for Christ will last, then tell me why are we more concerned about being recognized by the creation than the **creator**? We should be asking the creator questions about ourselves when He *re-presents* things in our lives.

The words *remonstrance* and *expostulation* are words that continue to explain *re-present*. God had me to look up these words also. Remember the word of God tells us when we read, read with understanding, *(.....and with all they getting get understanding, Proverbs 4:7)*. In plain simple language, God's word is saying this; God wants you to have an understanding. Understanding is vital to human nature to continue in the development and the progressions of this life. He (GOD) just doesn't want you to have **your understanding.** This is why we must consult God about our life. This simple but powerful principle not only pertains to just the bible, but to all things that cause us to get understanding or increase in knowledge. Hold on to your seat belt for this definition. You will see yourself in the meaning of these words, pleading your case to God while He keeps *re-presenting* the truth about you to *you.*

I know I am in the right

Remonstrance means *to say or plead in protest, objection or reproof; object completely; to show; to warn; opposition. Expostulation* means **to** *reason earnestly with someone in an effort to dissuade or correct; to demand strongly.* This is what Job was doing while God was showing him his character flaws. In Job 13:3, 13-18 The New Bible: "*But my dispute is with God, not you; I want to argue my case with him. Be quiet and give me a chance to speck, and let the results be what they will. I am ready to risk my life. I've lost all hope, so what if God kills me? I am going to state my case to him. It may even be that my boldness will save me, since no wicked man would dare to face God. Now listen to my words of explanation. I am ready to state my case, because **I know I am in the right**.*" Job had already taken his stand of being right and was willing to risk his life on his own self-righteousness. He enters into the presence of God with a closed spirit toward God correcting, showing, or reproofing him. **It was his understanding**. In Job's mind, he was right and God was wrong. What a dangerous state of mind to be in while in God's presence. Job's body and spirit were in distress. He was suffering the anguish of not understanding why this had to happen to him. Depression was followed with anger because in Job's mind, he did all the things **he** thought God wanted him to do. How many times have we been there? Mad at the Father after doing **all** we thought He wanted us to do?

Job had lost everything and this horrific condition of his body would not leave. God re-presents the truth back to us over and over again and we just don't get it. He portrays us in His light and shows us the naked truth about our flaws in our character. We need to stop comparing ourselves to other people and start looking for the light of God to shine in our dark places of integrity. Let's stop pointing the finger at other people when God is shinning His light directly on us. There once was soundness, completeness and unity; we were a ground fit for the master's use. Now, there is only a desolate land of division, full of fragments of what use to be holy in our lives. Holiness was evident in our lives. But holiness is replaced by self-deception and what feels good to me. Indignity has turned into mortification a feeling of shame, humiliation, or wounded pride. These are the hidden things we don't want anyone to know about us. But like Job, God knows they are there and He keeps re-presenting them to us.

we know better than God

We debate most of what God tells us about our lives. We argue, plead and justify our case as if we know better than God. We forget the word of God is for the reproof and correction, to show, to warn and to make clear in the minds of His children what our purpose is in God. In 2 Timothy 3:16-17 we can read this truth, "*All scripture is given by inspiration of God, and is profitable for doctrine, for reproof, for correction, for instruction in righteousness; That the man of God may be perfect, thoroughly furnished unto all good works."* We were made for His glory, not ours. Even our thoughts betray us in God's presence. We speak one thing in prayer but think another that is so far from His word. Yes, He knows the very thoughts and intents of our heart, even when we pray. So why are we arguing with God when He re-presents something back to us about our lives?

It really is ALL about Him, His word, and His glory. Our purpose is to find man's righteousness and destiny in God, not in man or woman. Job was in a state of complaining and he objected strongly with God about what was happening to him, his wife, children and his livelihood. Yes, this is a good example of the word *remonstrance.* Change came and there was no explanation given to the *why me Lord?* How many times have we asked God that question? How dare God come and disrupt and interfere in our lives without first asking us? Who does He think He is? *God the creator of all things...... maybe?* We all have been argumentative with God at one time or another in our lives, so we can understand how our brother, Job, felt. We have felt the abandonment of God's presence when a loved one has died unexpectedly or our mother or father leaves us in foster care with the promise of returning someday........... but that day never came. We ask God questions when we suffer the loss of a job or while going through the failure to move on after a bitter divorce. For some, we question God and ask if we should stay in a marriage that seems love-less and full of yesterday's hurts for the sake of the children. Or perhaps we say to God, "I am now in my 40's or 50's and where is my spouse or the promotion I've been praying for all these years?" Or "God, why did my business go into bankruptcy and where have you been all my life?" We want God to change our circumstances quickly and immediately. We don't want Him wasting our time asking us endless questions we don't comprehend or even realize exist. Our battle cry is "fix it **NOW!"**

When God re-presents our life to us, we cry out and we want Him to move instantly. But when it comes to us making changes, we want Him to have patience with us while we move like snails in changing our character according to His word. We come up with all sorts of excuses why we can't do what He has said in His word. An older friend told me this about excuses, "They are cousins to a lie." Excuses have some form of the truth in them, but enough of a lie to get you out of any situation if worded properly, and YES, we know how to do that well. We have an excuse carefully worded for everything God represents to us in life, including our bad choices. We offer excuses about our choices and keep complaining but we refuse to do what He said in His word. Then comes the anger.

Job complained too

Our brother Job complained and protested to God and the friends that would listen to him from chapter one to thirty-seven. **Then God had enough**. It is a terrible thing to be in the hands of an angry God. We must be careful what we say to our Father, even when we are hurting and angry with him. Yes, as children of God, we do get angry with our heavenly Father just like our kids get angry with us. However, He is God enough to handle misplaced anger towards Him that should be channeled toward ourselves or the devil. There is always a reason why God's purpose must be fulfilled in our lives, whether we understand it or not. Our understanding is NOT a prerequisite in God's decision making. How great He is! His power is absolute! His understanding is unlimited. This is what we must understand. God is God!!

In the book of Job, our Father speaks to our brother:

"Then out of the storm the Lord spoke to Job. Who are you to question my wisdom with your ignorant, empty words? Stand up now like a man, and answer the questions I ask you. Were you there when I made the world? If you know so much, tell me about it. Who decided how large it would be? Who stretched the measuring line over it? Do you know all the answers? What holds up the pillars that support the earth? Who laid the cornerstone of the world? In the dawn of that day the stars sang together, and the heavenly beings shouted for joy. Who closed the gates to hold back the sea when it burst from the womb of the earth? It was I who covered the sea with clouds and wrapped it in darkness. I marked a boundary for the sea and kept it behind bolted gates. I told it, so far and no farther! Here your powerful waves must stop. Job, have you ever in all your life commanded a day to dawn? Have you ordered the dawn to seize the earth and shake the wicked from their hiding places? Daylight makes the hills and valleys stand out like the folds of a garment, clear as the imprint of a seal on clay. The light of day is too bright for the wicked and restrains them from doing violence. Have you been to the springs in the depths of the sea? Have you walked on the floor of the ocean? Has anyone ever shown you the gates that guard the dark world of the dead? Have you any idea how big the world is? Answer me if you know. Do you know where the light comes from or what the source of darkness is? Can you show them how far to go, or send them back again? I am sure you can, because you're so old and were there when the world was made!

Job was questioning God and that is not a bad thing.

there is a time to question God

I remember older people telling me when I was younger, "You should never question God." I differed from that statement even then, I just had sense enough not to argue with my elders. I believe one can ask God anything with the proper attitude and respect. If you can't ask God, then who can you ask? He's the creator of all the answers because He alone creates. God is a speaking God and He is speaking to us all the time through His Spirit. He has given us the ability to speak to mankind but most of all, to Him. He takes pleasure and delight in His children asking Him any question and them waiting patiently to hear what He has to say. The problem is not in the asking, it is in your approach. Go ahead, ask God that tough question and wait on the answer, but be careful how you approach Him.

Approaching God in the wrong attitude or posture like Job did, can be life threatening to you and to your loved ones. We must take a humble or meek position in the presence of one greater than our self. In 1 Peter 5:6, God's word says, *"Humble yourself under the mighty hand of God and in due time He shall exalt you."* This is why He says, God sets Himself against the proud and haughty, but gives grace [continually] to the lowly, those who are humble enough to receive it. Our father still loves us even when we approach Him in the wrong way. But like a parent, we may be disciplined for coming to Him in the wrong posture.

I approached God in the wrong way when I started to complain about the way my life was going. Like Job, I had a list of things I complained about daily. I hated my job as a retail manager. I was working long hours and missing out on so much of my children's lives. I would come home tired after lifting heavy boxes because I was relocating departments within the store. My frustration came from dealing with rude customers, paper work, mark downs, mark ups, and keeping my daily sales quotas up. These were just a few of my everyday tasks and they were just the tip of the iceberg. Since I was a working mom, I had another full time job to deal with at home.

everybody wanted more........

When I came home there was homework that needed to be checked. Whether I or my husband would do it would depend on who would win the argument or who would make the time. There were also bathrooms that needed to be cleaned or supervised while our children cleaned them. There was food that needed to be cooked or brought home. My husband and I would take turns doing most of the cooking, only after thinking why can't the other person do this. When our kids got old enough to help with the cooking and cleaning, it somewhat eased the load of doing it, but not all the arguments. There was a list of places the kids needed to be dropped off and then later picked up; like football practice, trips to the mall and church on weekdays, just to mention a few. Someone had to drive them and then pick them up too. Clothes that must be washed in order for the family to have something clean to wear. We had to go to PTA meetings at my children's schools, which I hated. We would rather call the teacher and set up an appointment to see them than spend two or three hours at the school. Like Job, I complained to God about life as a mom and then there were all my personal issues that I had not forgiven my husband for.

My husband had a list of cruel and insensitive words he said to me when I somehow failed him. And I allowed him to plant those negative words deep inside my spirit and they hurt me to my soul. There were days I would rather stay late and work a twelve hour day than come home to him and the demands of my family. I felt like my husband and family only wanted to take from me. I felt like he had nothing to give to me but negative words. I found more comfort in a pillow wrapped in plastic in the pillow aisles of my department than in my own bed with my husband. I only got more demands and negative words from him. The money I was making was great. With my husband being in the Air Force, we could pay the bills and then have some left over............right? Not so. We were making more money, but we still had nothing left at the end of the month.

My brother-in-law, Louis, said this to us in the early days of our marriage that later became a fact of life for us, "The more money you make means the more money you will spend." The hole in our money bag just got bigger and bigger. The more money we earned meant the more money we needed. There were so many things we had waited all of our lives on and we felt we deserved them so we brought them. We were like so many people today caught in a vicious cycle of finances. In Haggai 1:6-7 it's very plain, *"You plant much but harvest little. You have scarcely enough to eat or drink, and not enough clothes to keep you warm. Your income disappears, as though you were putting it into pockets filled with holes! Think it over, says the Lord of Hosts. Consider how you have acted, and what has happened as a result!"* No matter what, we never had enough money and everyone wanted more from me.

CHAPTER SEVEN

God, you promised

I would give all but twenty dollars of my pay check to the bills and somehow we still couldn't pull ourselves out of debit. There would be days I would be so angry at God and my husband. Why my husband? I choose to blame him just like Adam did with Eve in the Garden of Eden. Who else in the home carries the responsibility of maintaining the finances besides me? I would tell God we paid our tenth and we sowed a seed according to your word, so why haven't we got out of debt yet? We both would go months without buying ourselves anything. I would carry my lunch to work or not eat at all so I wouldn't spend the money. Meanwhile, I was getting angrier and angrier at my husband because we were still in debt. My hair would start falling out before I would get a relaxer. Nothing seemed to help us with our finances and the arguing with my husband got more intense. Like Job, I questioned God and I was angry. I would say, "God you told us if you want to get out of debt, then sow a financial seed in good ground. Lord, we have been doing that principle since we understood it but to no avail for us," or so I thought at that time. God knew I loved Him with all my heart and He knew I would always pay my tenth to Him no matter what was going wrong in the finances. I knew He could turn our money flow into a river at any point in His timing. But like Job, I still kept questioning God and getting more and more frustrated. We were living in a desert place spiritually and where were God's promises?

The bible proclaims God's ability to bring water to the dry places in our lives and ours were as dry as the Arizona dessert I grew up in. In Psalms 105:41-45, God's word says "*He opened up a rock, and water gushed out to form*

56

a river through the dry and barren land; for he remembered his sacred promises to Abraham his servant. So he brought his chosen ones singing into the Promised Land. He gave them the lands of the Gentiles, complete with their growing crop: they ate what others planted. This was done to make them faithful and obedient to his laws. Hallelujah!" I knew what God had promised us but I was not seeing the promises in our lives. God kept speaking to me through books, tapes and sermons. But there were days I listened to the devil more than I listened to my Father. I too have approached my Father the wrong way just like brother Job did. I got answers from the creator that humbled me instantly and my tears fell like the water of a waterfall. I wasn't ready for a godly change in my life, but I knew not to approach my Father like that again. God still kept *re-presenting* my life to me.

Chapter 8

The silent treatment from God

I
t was like He was re-introducing the reality of who I was so I could make a choice or a decision to move in *NOW*. Have you ever got the silent treatment from God when you have been disobedient to what He has told you to do? I would rather God speak and correct me right then and there, than have Him withhold His words. When the Father withholds His words, it's like He is refusing to embrace you with His arms. If He is speaking, then I know what He wants me to do. But if He stops speaking, then there is no instruction on what I must do. I am left with my own thoughts and not His. I am left trying to understand God in a life-time journey and it becomes even harder in the absence of His (instructions) words. Psalms 32:7-8 says this: *"Thou art my hiding place; thou shalt preserve me from trouble; thou shat compass me about with songs of deliverance. I will instruct thee and teach thee in the way which thou shalt go; I will guide thee with mine eye."* If we listen to our Father, He

will lead us into the *NOW* of our life but He is not rude. His silence says He will not argue with you but He has not stopped loving you.

By the 40th chapter, Job had a new attitude. The change God wanted to see had taken place in his integrity. He became "whole and complete; lacking nothing." Job's change moved him to a transformation of him laying down his old nature and putting on God's nature. Our brother Job doesn't quite recall when the exact moment of change turned into a transformation. In the 40th chapter of Job, God asks this question,

> *"Job, you challenged Almighty God; will you give up now, or will you answer? I spoke foolishly, Lord. What can I answer? I will not try to say anything else. I have already said more than I should. Then out of the storm the Lord spoke Job once again. Stand up now like a man, and answer my questions. Are you trying to prove that I am unjust to put me in the wrong and yourself in the right? Are you as strong as I am? Can your voice thunder as loud as mine? If so, stand up in your honor and pride; clothe yourself with majesty and glory. Look at those who are proud; pour out your anger and humble them. Yes, look at them and bring them down; crush the wicked where they stand. Bury them all in the ground; bind them in the world of the dead. Then I will be the first to praise you and admit that you won the victory yourself."*

Job's approach had changed and God began to answer his questions.

Now that his approach had changed, the loving Father began to reveal things to His child Job. In chapter 42, Job comes to his senses like those of us who really fear and respect our heavenly Father.

"Then Job answered the Lord. I know, Lord, that you are all powerful; that you can do everything you want. You ask how I dare question your wisdom when I am so very ignorant, I talked about things I did not understand, about marvels too great for me to know. You told me to listen while you spoke and to try to answer your questions. In the past I knew only what others had told me, but now I have seen you with my own eyes. So I am ashamed of all I have said and repent in dust and ashes (1-6)."

Job's understanding of God was becoming clear. His situation had not changed but Job had. Job now knew a different side of God and he had a new relationship with God. There is one thing to hear other people talk about God, but it is a different ball game when you get to play ball with our heavenly Father as the pitcher. This produced God's understanding in Job.

letting go of my understanding

God had me to write this simple poem when I was letting go of my understanding and was willingly holding on to His understanding with all my life. He kept *re-presenting* my life back to me and giving me answers to the "What's" and to the "Whys" of my life existence. It did not matter whether they were good or bad, I *NOW* was ready to hear them. The poem goes like this: *"I was sitting on the edge of my world, and God pushed me off, my arms weren't flapping, but my spirit was clapping, saying GIRL WELCOME BACK FROM A LIE:......"* I believed the entire lie that was told to me of who I was and who I could never be. In my spirit, I gave up on life and their words echoed through my life. Then I died to the vision God had for me. Please take note of this: A vision is not fruit, it is only a seed of one's potential that must be cultivated and refined into good ground over many years before manifestation breaks forth. Life is full of lies about who we are and what we can never be.

We must start with the vision or the seed of our potential from God. God shows us the endless possibilities, or a window into what He has for us. It is like God himself showing you a glimpse or a foretaste of what He is willing to release into your care. *"Oh taste and see that the Lord is good..."Psalms 34:8!* Remember a vision is a seed with no fruit. It has the power to give life at the first taste of water. Keep in mind God is the **quintessential;** He is the essence that brings water to life. Without water or without God's watering of the seed, vision can't come forth. But in order for life to burst forth, the outer shell of the seed (You) must die. Our flesh must die in order to release the life giving force that lays dormant beneath our covering. God uses our falls (Humpty Dumpty) to re-present our life to us during our Remonstrance (complaining and protesting) to reveal the vision for our life. God wants us to examine our results in life based on our choices and take the time to examine what is being said about you.

I chose to believe the lie I was told about myself because I did make the choice to find out the truth. I became a self portrait of their words and they still weren't happy. My husband would tell me this on a regular basis, "You will not make it to heaven if you don't get rid of your unforgiveness, bitterness, and anger toward me and the rest of the people who have hurt you." Was my husband wrong in telling me this? NO! That is the word of God. The problem was "when" he would say it and "why" he was saying it. God's word was not meant to be a weapon to destroy His people or to be used to make a point in an argument. When that statement, and many others, were used to hit me in the middle of a heated war of words, I felt he sucker punched me. What do you say when the truth is thrown in your face at a hundred miles per hour? It left me naked and ashamed. My spirit was thrown back each time he would make these kinds of statements in the midst of an argument. How do you then dispute God's word in the midst of a personal battle? You don't. I would find something in his past and throw it at him, so he too could feel the same pain I was feeling from the words he would use toward me. It was a fact but still a lie.

when you start fighting people, you stop fighting the enemy

The lie about who I was had become very believable because I was living it. My husband and I were two children lost in a maze called marriage. Our examples we had seen were our parents and their marriages. Their marriages were filled with dysfunctional habits, disorder, and confusion also. This was a result of what they had seen in their parent's marriages. Both of our parents learned how to <u>survive </u> and not thrive in their marriage. We were headed down that same road of survival. A child can only become what they are taught and shown in their upbringing. Until that child has a chance to be exposed and experience something different, they will become a product of their surroundings. In other words, an adult is only a grown up child developed from their environment and choices. Therefore, our marriage was a product of our background and our good and bad choices we saw in our parents and those around us. Choice can be a powerful element in our environment. A choice gives us the power to stop *anything*, even the chaos in our marriages if we would just choose to stop the discord.

This chaos went on for many years of my marriage. I didn't know who I was and I didn't like what my parents, husband, children, and job wanted me to become. So the battle of wills was on in my life. I find it very funny that people can tell you about what you are suppose to be, but don't have a clue who they are. I heard what I thought was the truth coming out of my husband's mouth, no matter how painful it may have seemed at the time. I gave his words the power to alter my life's journey from heaven to hell on earth. His words felt like boulders falling from the sky crushing me to death, but I just wouldn't die. The words from my husband were like my mother's words confirming that I was no use to anyone. In the midst of arguments, he criticized my cooking calling it garbage. Then went on to my clothes and how he didn't like them. If I had changed jobs recently, I was told I was no help to him financially. My motherhood was criticized and he wasn't getting enough sex in the bedroom. The list of negative words between us went on and on in our marriage. Some of the things he said *I became*, but none of it was the **truth** about me.

Even though these things had manifested in my life, it was not who I was. By this time, I remembered just where I laid down my cussing spirit and gladly picked it up. I released it with the uttermost precision to destroy him like he was trying to destroy me. It was at those times I thought he was the enemy and not the man I thought I married. The words he was choosing to say to me was ripping away what love I had for him. This left me with what I thought was my only choice and that choice was to cuss him out with words of destruction, rather than to bless him. Some of our verbal confrontations were as bloody as the war in Iran. But the causalities were our children, wounded and dysfunctional from not having the proper love in the home. The power of **now** was no where in sight, because yesterday and all of its problems were occupying the space.

The verbal fighting would sometimes go on into the night and early morning with us both trying to explain our points of view, as if it was the truth about each other. I let loose on him the rage I felt toward my mother and any one else who tried to control me. I unleashed the rage of past hurts and pains until I could not think of any more words that might bring me pleasure while telling him off. Anything I could think to say that would hurt him, I used it. I knew this anger well and it became one of my many friends that traveled within me. This rage and anger had enveloped me on a daily basis.

This anger and rage was ageless and unpredictable. It's job was to build a wall of protection around my hurts and pains and not let anyone in or out. I needed a **now** word from God. Yes, I would view my husband as the enemy, as well as others who I thought were trying to hurt me. Yes, there were times he would reach out to me, but all I could see were weapons that were formed against me. Once I put a face on my pain, I realized this battle I was fighting would be won by the devil. **When you start fighting people,**

you stop fighting the enemy. After a bloody war of words, my husband would spend many days trying to help me with words of encouragement. He would try desperately to show me how to overcome my feelings of inadequacy. He would begin spending money on flowers and cooking me special dinners again. In peace times at home, my husband would do all of these things and more without one complaint.

I would sit thinking and watching my husband doing things around the house for me after one of our many arguments. I would ask myself why is he now so attentive to my needs and how long will this behavior last. He was like so many men (if women would let them) who would talk about the issue *one time and one time* **only**. Then the issue that was argued is to be swept under the proverbial rug never to be spoken of again. Whether he understood what he has done.....or what I have done......or what the both of us have done in the relationship. The issue is to go under the proverbial rug along with the pain and the confusion it caused. This leaves most women wanting to talk about the issue more than once, twice or however long it takes to find closure. While the man, on the other hand, has nothing more to say about the argument and will become defensive if asked to continue talking. What most men don't understand is that it was *words* from one party or both that cause the pain. And it will take the **repeating** of *words* to begin the healing process, not the absence of them. How does a man except a woman to be *intimate* sexually with him, when she can't be *verbally* intimate with him. Remember men, a woman finds trust in your words not in the size of your pants. In the Bible it states this about our words, *"A man hath joy by the answer of his mouth: and a word spoken in due season, how good it is,"* (Proverbs 15:23).

Sometimes, my husband acted as if the family owed him our lives for his participating and providing for the family. This left me feeling like we couldn't please him no matter what we did or didn't do. I felt like I was in a no win situation and needed someone to help me NOW. During the peaceful times, my husband was helpful and caring. He was very attentive to my words and feelings. We would go on one and two day vacations to Myrtle Beach; money was no object then. He would even take me out on dates. But once our guard was down, the devil would launch an all out attack on the both of us to the point we would both regret showing our vulnerability toward each other. The devil had us believing the other person was the enemy. The devil was happy because we were fighting each other and not him.

God sends us someone to help us

The constant and steady arguing and not being able to find closure in any of the arguments kept our dysfunctional behavior alive for years. This was the door that *we* kept open for the devil to come in and out to continue to sow discord in our marriage and family. Dr Phil said this, "If you continue to do what you have always done. You will continue to get what you always have."

All the good seeds we both sowed into each other, we were more than willing to quickly remove them with our words and actions during times of verbal wars. Therefore, there wasn't much of a harvest left of compassion toward each other. After each cycle, I was left feeling like I could not let my guard down for anyone at anytime. Trusting loved ones was no different than anyone on the street. When my husband looked back on those years, he describes himself like this, "I wasn't a hero in your life but I wanted to help you so badly. The truth is, I was a little boy trying to figure out life myself. And no matter what I did, the anger, rage, arguing, bills, and rejection returned to our marriage." Remember God will always send help, but the problem is we don't always recognize it as help. The glasses of brokenness we wear, stops us from seeing the **true** help we need so desperately in our life-time. My help, and his, was there all the time but I could not see it because of my brokenness.

If you want to see your help, keep asking God to show it to you. I was watching the Oprah Show on one of my days off and she said something that stuck with me. It went something like this, "God will send someone in to your life to finish what He has started in the beginning. We must slow down long enough to figure out who that person(s) is." I went wow!! God sends people all around us to help us through life. Those persons I **now** know are my husband and children. Look around you and ask God to show you those persons He has sent to help you through life.

After the many wars we had, I would feel just as empty as I began. My husband's words from the past reminded me of a perfection I thought I couldn't reach in this life. This is why when I saw my baby son, I knew it may be the last chance to get it right with God and man. I reached for the hope and the love of God I found in my baby son. I asked God to please help me with this precious soul I called my "last chance." Help was somehow delayed because I refused to choose the *now* for years and all I had to offer my new son was the bleeding wounds of yesterday's hurts. I washed him and my other children in foul and tainted words on a daily basis in our home. When I was angry, anger came spewing out from my mouth like a volcano, destroying and distorting everything in my home. I didn't want to go to his football games because I couldn't find anything to wear that would cover up my overweight body. I sometimes didn't want to go because of the depressed state I was in. Just getting enough energy to brush my teeth was all I could do some days. I kept telling myself, you have to hold on to enough strength to go back to work and complete another 12 hour work day. Because I was running on empty, I felt I had nothing to give to anyone except myself.

I was existing in my life and then my husband told me how my son (age 8 to11) would cry because I was rarely there to cheer him on at his football games. What mother wouldn't want to be there to support her child? Does this truly mean I didn't love him like the other mothers and fathers who were there? This left me feeling even more inadequate as a mother and as a wife. Torment went to a new level in my life. It was like opening a closet that was once full of the finest clothes ever made and then finding only one garment of disgrace, shame, embarrassment, and inadequacies to wear. Then saying to yourself, "If this is all I have to work with, let me try to make it work." I was giving what I could to make it work but my spirit was empty. I believe the reason behind my husband telling me about our son and so many other problems in our marriage was to prove that he was right about what he was saying about me. I felt he was more concerned about the changes he wanted to see in me, than the changes he needed to change in himself. We both played the blame game and were loosing ourselves and our children. Because no one wins in the blame game, we all become losers in one way or another. These were all symptoms of an empty spirit.

Chapter 9

An empty spirit

Yes, depression is a symptom of an empty spirit, and my spirit was as empty as a desert. I was left with the imprints of what was left in my life. Mothers give until we have nothing left to give. Mothers give of our essentials, the part that keeps us alive. We give from the river of our own essence, meaning our identity, ingredients, or the crucial element that make us person. Yes, mothers are people too. We are people with dreams and visions before we became wives and then later mothers. Mothers give up their dreams and visions so that their family might live and not die. The schooling she needs to finish is put on hold until there is a way to find money in an already tight budget. But somehow, that day never seems to come. The dreams her parents had for her seem to fly away like a beautiful bird going off into the sunset. Those dreams will never be seen or heard of again. The book that she was going to write that captured her imagination and passion is **now** a small journal of notes. It has become a pile of passing thoughts on bits and pieces of paper stuck inside a folder. The business she desperately wanted to start has become nothing but a list of excuses why she hasn't even tried. Most mothers are in a state of depression and don't even know it. They have given so much of their essential parts that depression and an empty spirit become a way of life.

Many mothers find themselves void of anything to give and they are tired. If you find yourself like I did, pushing away your children and loved ones, please keep on reading because help is just on the next page. I found myself pushing my youngest son away like the other children I had. I retreated back to my room, like my father did for years. We were only allowed in his room to bring food and drink. If we dare to enter his room, he would want to talk about himself for hours rather then to take one moment to listen to us. Have you ever found yourself in a place where you only want to talk about your problems daily? What you are experiencing is called an empty spirit. Your spirit is full of yesterday's unforgiveness and the pain it has caused you. You're choosing to hold on to the past and all the problems that surrounded the circumstances of that dilemma. You must tell your mind and your emotions you are no longer there. The **now** has done nothing to you and it waits on the edge of it's seat to give you your life back. God told me this while I was trying to find my **now,** "Tangela, why hold on to a memory of life, when you have life?" As a result of some of my childhood experiences, God helped me to write this poem about unforgiveness.

THE PAIN OF UNFORGIVING

When the pain of unforgiving, is more than I could ever bear,
*I turn my eyes up to Jesus, and cry out **"ARE YOU***
EVEN THERE!!!"

I ran calling to my mother, like sometimes we all do

Who would help me on this day when I'm going through.

She took one long look at me and slowly dropped her head and said;

"I cannot help you my daughter when my heart is already dead."

I ran quickly out the door again to try and find my father,

When suddenly I felt my heart stop and I realized I would be nothing but a bother.

I sat down where I was and wondered how did all this pain begin?

Was it because I was selfish and unwilling to forgive...thinking only of my pain??? Oh God, who would give me a hand?

I looked up and saw this man name Jesus, he showed me nailprints in his hands. I said, "Jesus, who put those nails there?"

He just looked at me with his crown of thorns and a broken heart,

With this spear stuck in his side and said,

"Tangela my daughter, **You're the reason why I died."**_

The cycle of depression, going from one generation to the next, was planted deeply inside of me. I was giving birth to the next generation, which was my children. In the midst of my depression, God began to speak to me. God said,

> *"Tangela, you are missing in action. You have retreated to your bedroom like a child on punishment. Haven't I told you that parents are the most important people in a child's surroundings? This is why I have created parents; to teach, to correct, to love, to discipline, to edify and to exhort my next generation. I AM the*

teacher of life's lessons, but my hands of healing and correction come from parents or loved ones in a child's life. Parents are the first understanding of authority in a child's environment. There must be an understanding or respect for authority at a young age in the child's upbringing. Otherwise, when that child becomes an adult, authority becomes something they fight against and do not embrace. Parents are the schoolmasters of life. They are my living examples, like Christ was when I made him flesh. He was the word walking among us to show us a more perfect way. Tangela you are suppose to be a more perfect way. An epistle read by your children and then the world. Please don't get the two mixed up because ministry starts at home and then to the world. This can not be achieved if you isolate yourself from your child and put up walls of anger to keep people at bay. Playing games with your children, you don't do that anymore. Being creative with the talent I have given you for making African art, you don't do that anymore. You would rather shoot yourself in the head than talk to your husband. You keep telling me this would be less painful and more meaningful. All you do is go to work and church. Where is the fun, the joy, the peace in doing that? Tangela, you have become a prisoner in your own life. Life now dictates to you, instead of you dictating to LIFE."

I was depressed, confused and angry but God was still speaking to me. God was re-presenting my life back to me again and the word confirmed where I was.

a people robbed and spoiled

I became what the scripture in Isaiah 42:22 says, *"But this is a people robbed and spoiled; they are all of them snared in holes, and they are hid in prison houses: they are for a prey, and none delivereth; for a spoil, and none saith, Restore."* To better understand this scripture and how it became my lifestyle over time, let's walk together into the biblical understanding of the word, *spoil*. The meaning of *spoil* is **to diminish in strength, value, quantity, and character**. I was freely giving satan permission to take my life away one hour, one minute, one second, one **now** at a time. I remember going to one of my counseling sessions and hearing the counselor say these words, "You have backed up a U-haul to your house and started filling it with all the promises and blessings of God. Then you and your husband just wave good-bye to the van as satan drove away with everything you ever hoped for. He leaves you and your husband with nothing but a dream of a better life." Satan was spoiling our lives.

The word makes the promises of God very plain if you are a tithe giver and give a costly offering according to the Holy Spirit. That costly offering must be more than just **money**. In Malachi 3:10-11 the word says, *"Open you the windows of heaven and pour you out a blessing, that there shall not be room enough to receive it. And I will rebuke the devourer for your sakes, and he shall not destroy the fruits of your ground."* In other words, God wants you to spend more time in asking Him to restore you, than giving the devil permission to destroy or spoil you. The bottom line is God wants your **time** as an offering also. Your time is more valuable than your money. Man can give you more money, but only God can give you more time. Your time is more priceless and precious than gold. Time can only be given once. Time is the part of us that can not be replaced. Time can only be replaced or redeemed by God. We try to give God everything else but our time. Satan wants to spoil our promises by stealing our time. Yes, some of us go to church on a regular basis. The pastor knows our name and the seat we sit in. But are we really there in spirit? Or are we just filling a physical square in time called **church service**? That is exactly what it is, a service we do unto a building and not to our Father. We are physically there but satan is stealing our **time with God**.

I did not have time for God

We might squeeze God into our morning with a quick hello or a very fast prayer. Then we are into the shower and out the door. If we didn't find time in the morning, then we say a prayer over our food at lunch. The food lasts longer in us than the half prayer we said over it. We don't have time for God in our day, however, if we put God first, we will never have a bad day again in our lives. Yes, some days may be more challenging than others. But the understanding or knowledge that your Father "got your back" and you trust in Him, makes all the difference in the world. When we choose not to give Him our time, earth then becomes the battle ground for satan to kill, steal, and destroy. The door for satan to destroy our marriage, jobs, and children is opened. I did not have time for God in my life but satan had walked thru the open door of life and brought in destruction.

Satan was spoiling my life and I was wasting away at the very thought of it. Life had no more pleasure for me, and the taste of it soured in my stomach. Life became a chore, something I had to do. It became burdensome, a routine of daily tasks, of things I needed to do and people to see. It was like going to the bathroom and having a bowel movement, and not caring enough to wipe. Life stunk like the waste that came out of my bowels; it only became a necessary function. The word **spoil** gets even deeper than that for me. I became tainted, rotten, and unfit for use. Yes, I was decaying from the inside out and the smell was foul in my father's nostrils. In Isaiah 3:24-26 it states, *"Instead of smelling of sweet perfume, they'll stink; for sashes they'll use ropes; their well-set hair will all fall out; they'll wear sacks instead of robes. All their beauty will be gone; all that will be left to them is shame and disgrace. Their husbands shall die in battle; the women, ravaged, shall sit crying on the ground,"* (The Way Bible). I didn't see myself as beautiful. The clothes I wore, I didn't care if they matched. I was going bald on both sides of my head. My spirit was crippled and I felt no completeness within the inner core of myself.

What happened to the unity I had with the Father, Son, and the Holy Spirit? They were my only hope of perfection in this life. They seemed to be taken away by the forcefulness of my **past**. It was as if hell opened her mouth and swallowed the last glimmer of light in a dark room called **my life**. GOD then reminded me that He came to give life and that more abundantly. He asked again what is **now**? I had no answers. I had no understanding of what He was asking me. So I did like most people do when asked a question they aren't sure of; I went to the dictionary. I was praying that somehow the answer would miraculously change the cycle of depression and move me into a life full of joy. I then reminded myself that over the course of my life, I have helped so many women find GOD and get reconnected to Him. Maybe **now** it's my turn.........

take the time to hear the father's voice

The Webster's dictionary defines **now** as: *in the time immediately before the present; in the time immediately to follow: the present time or moment; existing.* This made no sense to me at all. There was no great understanding or discernment; spiritual enlightenment didn't come rushing into my dark world of depression. It seemed as if my cries for help to my Father's throne could not be heard from the earth I stood on. It left me wondering why the creator would ask me a question and not give me an answer. So I did like any child would do, I asked my Father for the answer. This is His answer. This is my journey of self-discovery of the **now**. God already knows and has counted and numbered the many **nows** and presents in man's life span. All we need to do is walk them out.

GOD told me this, "*The greatest JOURNEY man will ever take, will be the WORD of GOD traveling from his head to his heart.*" This is truly a heart issue that man has to travel through. In Proverbs 4:23 it says this, "*Keep thy heart with all diligence; for out of it are the issues of life.*" What God told me and showed me changed my life. It changed the way I think and the way I see things forever. I know I will never be the same again and neither will anyone else who reads and understands what the Father is saying. If you take the time to hear the Father's voice through these pages, you will never be the same again.

I give thanks and honor to my heavenly Father for caring enough about me to reveal Himself to me. To send me the truth about who I am through His Son Jesus and His Holy Spirit, the teacher of all things. Thank you Father, from your daughter Tangela. So..........NOW WHAT???

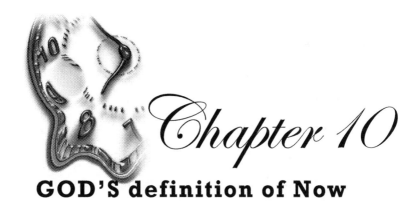

GOD'S definition of Now

In the next few chapters we will be discussing **now, destiny (future) and the past** while assigning meaning to each of them. Let's start with the obvious, what is **now** and how can we understand this one simple word. This one word can change your life like it did mine. This is God's definition of **now** that He gave me, "*Now is when the **past** of your life collides or comes together with the **future** of your **destiny**.*" This collision reproduces a specific purpose or place in time, called **now**. This leads you to the "presence of your life." Pastor Caleb Pierce said it like this, "**Now** is the ending of one thing and the beginning of another." It is the conclusion of a matter or the settling of an issue in ones mind and spirit. **Now** is the closing of one door and the opening of another. In your **nows**, you can choose to go towards your future goals, or you can choose to stay in your past. This power of choice is all left up to the individual person to make in every **now** of their lifetime, (We will talk more about *lifetime* later). Your lifetime is a collection of **nows** but we have some misconceptions about what **now** is.

Now is not just another fleeting moment in our lives. **Now** is not like the steam that is released from a tea pot. Steam escapes from the pot and later dissipates into the atmosphere, never to be heard from or seen again. **Now** has great substance and profound meaning in itself. **Now** waits for the person to recognize the importance of their **now**. Then it gives them another **now** to do something different with their life. Everything in your life will start from a decision you have made in your **now,** not in your **past**. Now ask the same question that many of us do each and everyday, "**Now**…….what do I do with this?"

NOW is right after your past, but before your future

Now doesn't have the ability to change anything without the help of your choice. The job of **now** is to keep re-presenting itself to you until you are ready to exercise your God given authority to change. *Now* is right after your **past**, but before your **future**. *NOW* is an appointed or a set place of time in your life. *NOW* is looking at the reality of ones existence. When looking at your existence, you must decide whether to keep the reality you're looking at or to change it. *Now* is a holding position that God keeps us in. The holding position of **now** is a place where we can go forward into purpose or stay living in our past. This place is also a time for releasing and receiving from God, spouses, family members, and friends. God told me this about a true friend, "*A true friend helps you to discover life mysteries and an acquaintance takes away what you have discovered.*" Be very careful who you call your friends. Are they adding to your life or taking away what you have gained? Are they keeping you in the past or helping you move towards your purpose? You must make that decision.

Now is a place of decision making. *Now* is between your past and your future. *Now* can also be a place where our past comes and robs the first steps of a new beginning in a **now**. How many times has this happened to you? You make plans and promise yourself you would start something. But something always seems to get in the way of that promise you made in a **now**. However, in order to make the necessary changes or decisions, you need to be free from your past. Now that promise or plan becomes lost somewhere in time. That **now** decision then becomes your past. Then the feeling of giving up overwhelms your spirit. Failure takes over hope and hope dies a very slow and painful death. You start to say, "Why even bother?" The thought of beginning over becomes something you dread instead of anticipate. So another *now* is missed in your life. But be of good cheer. If you miss this **now**, don't worry because God has another one waiting just for you. Once we understand the **now** that has passed, we have a choice to make.

your permission to start a new change

A **now** can be a profound point of understanding who we are and our purpose in life. **Now** is an entrance point or the birthing of change if we

choose to embrace it. In our **now** we can decide to change our lifestyle for the better or for the worse. **Now** is a pivotal point in our lives for change. A good example is after the death of a loved one. Death is but a fleeting or passing moment in our lives. It doesn't stay forever. The result of death can stay with us, but the spirit of death is only a moment or a second of our lives. Think about a car accident and how quickly death comes to take what was assigned to us. God comes into our **nows** for only a few brief seconds and takes us from what we know, to what is unknown to us. Death can only come and take what belongs to it and then it is done. Death will never return again for that person or persons. Remember, physical death is forever. God is the only one who can rob from death or the result of its aftermath. Then God brings a new **now** again. Regardless of the many things that happen in our lives, we can use our **nows** to decide to change our lives.

This new now brings new hope and faith to life again, if we would only receive it. Please keep this in mind, the moment after death is **life** and that more abundantly. That person(s) is dead but you're not! So, defeat death by living your life. You're still able to capture a perpetuating **now** if you would only release your spirit to live again. You're still alive and life is moving through your veins. This is where your life can begin a new **now.** Your spirit and mind must be focused on life without that person. They are gone and they will never return again. You must develop a lifestyle, habits, and new friends different from the past to what is **now**. Please take all the time you need. Let this discovering a new lifestyle for you become a *process* and not a project. The life of that person or persons and the impact they had on those around them has now turned into a spiritual memory. This memory is a diary written in the minds of their loved ones. The memories we will recall from our spiritual diaries will be the **nows** of their lifetime.

Have you ever really looked closely at a tombstone in a cemetery? Most tombstones record the first physical **now** which is the date the person was born and the *dash*. The tombstone also records their last **now** which is the date of their death. From conception until that person dies, God is the Lord of our **nows**. God alone is the beginning **now** and He is the ending **now**. Sounds simple and complete,....right? The sad and the most profound lettering on any tombstone is the *dash*. The dash presents our *life-time* from the time we were born until we die. The *dash* is all our **nows** imprinted on the stone for all physical life to see forever. The *dash* is our many perpetual or on going **nows** in our lives. It is the smallest of all the lettering on the tombstone. Even when the dash is read by the eye it still goes unnoticed on most tombstones, yet it is holds the most significance. This simple dash carries the seriousness or the importance of that person's life. The dash also shows their influence they had on this world or the lack of it. It represents what the person has accomplished, all the people they have met, and the mark they will leave on their loved ones. A simple dash represents what will last on humanity and in eternity. A dash can represent a stroke of a pen, if you were a writer. What literature will you leave behind for your loved ones and the world to read? If you are a floral designer, what designs will you leave as your signature pieces? A dash means **to complete, execute, or finish off hastily**. Is this the reason why we use the dash on a tombstone instead of a period? Have we *completed* the task at hand in our perpetual

nows given by God? Did we *execute* or carry out fully what was required by God for our lives? Did our **nows** *hastily* run out before we could finish or did we think another tomorrow was promised to us? The Bible has this to say about our lives, *"For what is your life? It is even a vapour, that appeareth for a little time, and then vanisheth away?" (James 4:14).*

Please remember no one can take those images away from you. They are imbedded into your imagination and replayed at will….. for a lifetime. A memory is nothing but a captured **now** replayed in the mind to console us. Remember, the love we feel towards our loved ones who have pasted on, is never lost. Why? Because it really wasn't love at all that we gave to them. Can you remember the first time you heard something might be wrong? Do you remember feeling a piece of you being torn or separated from your body? Some people feel a weakness in their knees or in their stomach. What we were feeling towards our loved ones was a piece of our energy being released. This energy is our life giving spirit that we received from God. Our time, power, force, vigor and liveliness are what we willingly released into their lives. When they passed on, they return the gift we call love back to us. This gives us back the energy we so badly need to live on. Why? God is much more than those forms of love. God is the energy that encompasses or personifies the spirit of love. Love is one of the many forms our energy can take on. We must know that their energy gives us permission to live on and live a full and fulfilling life without them. This is how we must live and stay in our **now** when a family member or loved one passes on.

This is where our spirit and mind must be focused on life. The life of the person who passed on and how they enriched our lives, is the memory we should be holding on to and not their death. Life leaves us with the memories of that person's past life to console us. Yes, **now** just sits there in a moment, waiting for your permission to start a new change. One has the choice to move forward or to re-live a past moment over and over again. Change can be the beginning thought of life or death. So we must start with changing our thinking in the **now**.

Those past memories can become death instead of life in our thoughts. We too will die a slow spiritual death from our thinking. We can choose those deadly thoughts or let them become the motivation we need to change our lives. Or we can continue the death process of our minds through our thoughts. Each day, we will be slowly dying in our thought life. The power of choice is all up to you. The power to change is in the next fleeting second of your decision. You must decide to live. The Hurricane disasters that happened in New Orleans in 2005 were a pivotal point for that city and its people. The people that lived there had to make hard decisions to leave their past life and all their belongings behind. They had to leave them to go in search of a **now** life somewhere in another state they knew nothing or very little about. Their lives *literally* rest in their next **now** decisions, hoping it would produce a new life for them and their families. Their **now** brought on a new change.

Now is a point of change for many people. The people of New Orleans experienced a sudden **now**. That **now** forced them to make hard choices they will have to continue to make. One **now** in our lives can change our reality for a lifetime. **Now** can be the beginning of a ripple in the waters of our lives. From that ripple comes many **nows** that will challenge our very foundation of who we are and what we believe in. It will make you ask your inner self the hard questions about life and God. Is God real? Does God stand by His word? Did Jesus really die on the cross for me and where is He **now**??? **Now** is the only time in your life where one can make decisions to change. **Now** is that spiritual sound we hear when change is knocking on our door. Do we open that door? Or leave it shut.

NOW doesn't blame anyone for anything

Your **now** can be an open door for you, not someone else, to make decisions. The decisions you make will establish or conclude your future. The Bible put it in these words in the latter part of 2 Chronicles 20:20, *"Believe in the Lord your God and you shall be established; believe and remain steadfast to His prophets and you shall prosper."* You must decide to act on what you believe and make a decision in your Now because your future will be established based on all your **nows**. One can not go around **now**. Your **now** is too big for you to **ignore**. How can a man pass through a minute, without first dealing with his present? You must deal with **now's** reality, whether you like what you see or not. **Now** doesn't go away. It is reborn quicker than you can blink an eye. **Now** is filled with all the hopes of a new life if we choose to move forward in it. Remember **now** won't just go away some day. It will be there until you sort through what is right and wrong with your life. **NOW** doesn't blame anyone for anything, it just presents itself to you and then asks you to make a choice to change.

Stop the blame game, because no one wins!! We all become losers and stay trapped in our past. If you choose to play the *blame game* it will cancel out your **nows**. The **now** and **blame** can't occupy the same space. One will always push out the other. Blame can leave you in a state of remorse, guilt and regret or with the feeling of not moving on with your life. Stop running from your **now**! If you're in prison, on drugs, divorced (again), lost a love one, sexually abused or whatever your problem might be at this present time, I implore you to please go and talk to someone who can help you find your way back to your **now.** Yes, you have tried counseling over and over again. And maybe it didn't work out for you. My words to you are try it again and again until it does work out. All you have to lose is your life, right? Isn't it worth it to keep trying until you run out of your **nows**? Either way, *you must stop the blame game.*

Chapter 11

God put our rectum behind us

Your life starts and ends in the **nows** of life. **Now** is not in our past-time or in our future. You can only find **now** in your **present**. Stop looking behind you when life is right in front of your face. The Bible says this, *"But this one thing I do, forgetting those things which are behind, and reaching forth unto those things which are before,"* (Philippians 3:13). The time it took you to read up to this point in the book is **now** over. You cannot change, alter or modify the past in anyway…….it's over……. it won't return unto you ever again. It is behind you….**Now** what are you going to do? What comes from behind us is not fit for our **now** lifestyle. This is why I believe God put our rectum behind us and not in front of us. We are to sit down, meaning quiet our spirit, relax and then release the foul substance that we have taken in from life.

Life leaves some foul things behind but we must release them. Have you ever seen the movie "Crash"? It is about people who didn't release life problems and the stresses that come with living an everyday life. They were filled with anger, resentment, and bitterness they encountered through their daily routine. Some had hidden discrimination they knew nothing about. Others didn't care if people knew it or not. They lashed out at loved ones, people they knew, people they didn't know and didn't care to take time to know them. They all felt they had a right to carry these feelings with them until one day they "Crashed." **Are you about to crash?** If God created a way for our bodies to let go of the waste we take in from day to day, then our spirits should be doing the same thing. The bible makes this point very clear. In Hebrews 12:1 it says this, "*Wherefore seeing we also are compassed about with so great a cloud of witnesses, let us lay aside every weight, and the sin which doth so easily beset us, and let us run with patience the race that is set before us.*" God didn't create man to carry weights (worries) around with him. Let it go!!!

These foul things, or weights, pollute our spirits and bodies to the point we can no longer hear from God. Somewhere along the way, we started relying on ourselves more and more to make decisions about problems that are too big for us to handle alone. It is a well known fact that stress and worries can cause high blood pressure, heart disease, strokes, and may other illnesses. Not releasing things or people is a symptom of unforgiveness. Unforgiveness over a long period of time can lead to cancer or mental retardation. Unforgiveness also causes depression and oppression if not released from our spirit at once. My heavenly Father told me this while in His presence, "*Unforgiveness is one of the greatest selfish acts that one can do to one self.*" My reply to my Father was for him to explain Himself. He then followed with this explanation, *"Forgiveness releases **your** spirit and not the person or persons who harmed you. This will Free you to praise and worship me in my presence where healing can begin and end."* Once you release it, God will flush it out of your life in His presence and release you to your next **now**. Let it go!!

Our **nows** are missed because of the spiritual waste we refuse to let go. How many people have you met with feces in their hands? Telling you they can't let it go because it is too painful for them. You and I both would look at that person like they have lost their mind. But do we still act like that spiritually? Do you wonder why people don't want to be around you? Is it because of the stuff you carry in your spirit **stinks**? Do you continue to talk about the same thing over and over again? Do you talk about those things year in and year out and not go find some help? If that's true, then you are carrying feces in your hands, telling people I refuse to wash my hands of this problem. Some people would rather talk about the feces in their hands over and over again, than just release it. The sad thing is that's what we look like in the spirit to God. We are holding on to what was intended to pass **through** us. Instead of using the toilet paper to wipe it away, some of us use our hands to carry it away. We carry the feces of life away with us when we worry and complain about our past or our future. So stop blaming, complaining, or worrying. Let it go!!

worrying is a sin

Did you know that worrying is a sin in the eyes of God. Some Christians get smart about what they call worrying. They use statements like:

I'm not worrying about that problem, I'm just being prayerful about it night and day;

I'm not troubled by it. I'm excising my faith by talking about it to you.

I'm not worried about it but it concerns me so I keep talking about it to let you know how I feel about it.

I'm not worrying about it but I don't think you understand what happened and what's going on.

I used all of these excuses and so many more to hide my lack of faith in God. God said this about worrying in Luke 12: 25-26,

> *"And which of you by being overly anxious and troubled with cares can add a cubit to his stature or a moment of time to his age (the length of his life)? If then you are not able to do such a little thing as that, why are you anxious and troubled with cares about the rest?"*

Also in Mathew 6: 33-34 the Bible says,

> *"But seek (aim at and strive after) first of all His kingdom and His righteousness (His way of doing and being right), and then all these things taken together will be given you besides. So do not worry or be anxious about tomorrow, for tomorrow will have worries and anxieties of its own. Sufficient for each day is its own trouble."*

This is one of many steps we must take to stay in the **now** of God. Worrying and complaining will always keep us from the presence of God.

Imagine the scripture saying this: Enter into His gates with complaining and into His courts with worrying. Believe me, that is not what the word says.

Instead of thanking God for our children that are alive, we complain because they won't listen to us. The truth is they are acting just like us when we didn't listen to our parents. We hate getting up out of a warm bed to go to a cold office, but we don't stop and appreciate the fact we have the ability to support our family and its lifestyle. We dislike some of our spouse's ways that make us go crazy just thinking about them, but when was the last time you really showed them just how much you love and depend on them. These are our **now** moments we miss because we refuse to let the waste **past** through us. Are we waiting for their **nows** to end before we tell them how much we love and value them? Only then will we find the reason to wash away the feces that was on our hands. Remember it came to **past,** not to stay for a lifetime. It is the blood of Jesus that can wash away anything that might stain our spirit. Nothing that comes out from behind us is fit for human consumption. So why do we keep re-living our *past* mistakes? God has our backs so we don't ever have to turn our eyes away from Him again. We can not lead our lives from behind. If we do that, we will fall once again in a different kind of feces. Wash away the feces from your past life and move on with your life in the **now**.

earthquakes challenge your decisions

God went on to say to me "**Now** is like an earthquake." Hebrews 12:27 says it like this, "*And this word, yet once more, signifieth the removing of*

95

those things that are shaken, as of things that are made, that those things which cannot be shaken may remain." Yes, there is an earthquake coming to many Godly homes awaking up their true purpose once again. In order to have an earthquake, there must be a *fault* somewhere in the earth, **you**. What does it means to have a **fault**? A *fault* is **a moral weakness, failing, a physical or intellectual imperfection or impairment; shortcoming in character, proneness to yield to temptation.** These and many others are the characteristics of most of our heros in the bible. They too had faults, but God still used them. There are faults in our systems.

Some of us make decisions knowing that it is not the direction our lives should be going in. These decisions lead to faults. Decisions like marrying the wrong person, doing drugs, drinking alcohol, and eating all the wrong foods but still wanting to lose weight. We have other decisions or faults like screaming at our children and then telling them not to disrespect you and other adults by raising their voice. Another example of a decision leading to a fault is smoking cigarettes, or other things, knowing each puff gets you a little closer to cancer. Or maybe you are abusing your spouse physically, verbally or even both. In Hebrew 12:27 it says, *"And this word" yet once more I am sending them to you for the removing of those things that are shaken (not ground in His principals) as of the things you have made in your life."* Let's stop blaming God and the devil for the choices we willingly made wrong in this journey called life. If you want something you never had, then you must do something you have never done.

Chapter 12

Some choices will cost you

The definition of insanity is doing the same thing over and over and again, but expecting something different. A decision is a profound choice that the members of our body must follow. God is shaking our choices as of the things that are made. What am I saying? We are the manifestation made from our choices in life. We are the product of our selection that we have chosen. If we choose to shoot and kill someone, the result from that action will be jail time. Your spouse and kids will be without a parent because of your choice to kill someone. If smoking is something you like to do and you won't give it up, don't be surprised that the butt you have been kissing is cancer. Your family will have to deal with the financial stress of trying to keep you alive. If you keep telling that man or woman to leave you and you don't want to be married to them anymore, please don't be angry when that person leaves. If you are looking for Mr. Right in all the wrong places, don't be shocked when you find

Mr. Wrong. Then, don't make the second mistake and marry him thinking you can change him for the better. What you purchase in the beginning of your relationship will be there at the end. God is trying to get us to take a look at some of our choices.

We make foolish choices every day of our lives. Some choices will cost us a lifetime of regret. Other choices are so small they go by unnoticed, yet we make them. It is the decision making process that God is coming after to change the wrong decisions that were **made** in our mind. The bible put it in these words in Isaiah 54:17, *"No weapon that is formed against thee shall prosper; and every tongue that shall rise against thee in judgment thou shalt condemn."* The statement "No weapon that is *formed* against thee shall prosper" is powerful. God then asked me this, "Tangela, have you ever seen a gun shoot and kill someone?" My answer was "yes, all the time on T.V. or at the movies." He then asked, "Did you *really* see the gun do that or was that a person making a choice for the gun?" Remember choices can be formed in the mind and then released as weapons to kill, steal and destroy. A choice can destroy a person or people and it happens all the time. It's called **war.** Just read the newspaper or look at the T.V. The power of one person's choice can change history for the better or for worse.

911 was a group of choices formed in the mind of many individuals to destroy as many people as possible in one day. It left the nation still trying to discover ways to protect us from bad choices other people might make against us. God has left it up to the individual to make those choices. This is why it is so very important that anything our Father didn't have a hand in making in our lives be **changed**. In changing our thoughts, according to our

Father's words, He promises us that every tongue that shall rise up against us in wrong judgment, He shall condemn. Remember, a child of God doesn't have to defend every negative thing said about them. This promise of His protection to defend His children is God's heritage in His word alone with His righteousness. He promised us not to have these crucial ingredients in our lives like this. Have you ever made a cake and foolishly forgot to put the eggs in and the cake simply fell apart? We too are just falling apart because we keep forgetting to put God in our every day life as the vital part of it. Blaming, unforgiveness, worrying and bad decisions are all the faults that lead to earthquakes in our lives. These are some of the reasons we refuse to operate in the **now** of our lives and start a new **now**. You must make the decision in the **now** and walk through the door of a new life.

NOW is a decision making door

Let's continue to look at what **now** is not. Your past or your future doesn't exist in your **now**. There is no room in **now** for ones past or future. Yes, we make decisions based on them, but **now** doesn't invite them in, we do. **Now** can only be our present; not our past or future. They all cannot cohabitate together in the same space in *time*. The **now** can only give birth to itself, reproducing another **now**, not another PAST or FUTURE, just another **now**. It is a place where one can make another decision to change for the better or worse. **Now** is a decision making door that opens to our future. Our future is birthed out of the **now** decisions we make every second of our lives. It is a place of decision.

In the bible, it makes this statement about a **now** choice we must make. It talks about how this choice will impact our future and the future of our children. Joshua 24:15 says, *"And if it seems evil to you to serve the Lord, choose for yourselves this day whom you will serve."* One must make decisions in **now** in order to get to your future. **Now** can be the porthole that one must discover through exploring and examining ones own lifestyle. When you examine your own existence, why God created you, you will find the porthole or the **now** in your life. Grab hold to that point in time where you stagnated. Usually we stagnate in the places we were hurt or destroyed. Look at the place where you wanted to give up. Then, ascertain (discover) a brand new reality (Now) that will reproduce life more abundantly. Then never let go of that new reality that was birthed out of a **now** for your life. If you don't know where you are going, then you will never understand where you are **now**. Your **past** is nothing but the process of life to get you to this place called **now**. To fully understand this statement, one must comprehend the word **destiny**.

Chapter 13

The throne of your *past*

I n this earthquake, there are two great faults colliding together and they are your past and God's **destiny** (future) for your life. In finding God's destiny for your life, one **cannot** hold on to the past or former things. It is just that, a PAST life you once had. Yesterday was a past life you lived. It was full of ALL your past mistakes, errors, mishaps, wrong judgments, etc; God loves man and woman so much, He creates another day for us to get our relationship right with him and then He waits patiently with open arms to receive us to Himself. Bishop George Bloomer made a statement that shook my foundation in one of his conferences. He said, "I am not my past. I have moved on and gotten a new address and I am a new creature made in the image of my true Father." The sad truth is I lived in the past for so many years. Let's take a look at what I lived in and refused to let it pass.

God gave me an understanding of Hebrew 12:27 back in 1998. I was returning from a four year tour in Germany. Germany was my Egypt; it was hell on earth for me. When I left America, I left all my comfort zones, hiding places, and friends I thought I could count on in the time of need. It was just me and God working it out. I kept stumbling at the truth about myself whenever God showed me my nakedness. I told him time and time again, it wasn't me, it was my mother, father, brothers, sisters, husband, or the many jobs that made me do the things I did. If "they" would just leave me alone or listen to me, then I wouldn't have to do or act the way I did. I am a nice, saved, and blessed person if people would just let me be. In other words, I kept on telling God it is everyone's fault why I am the way I am.

I became like Adam. I was blaming people and life for my actions that caused a brake in the fellowship I had with God. But just like Adam, God kept on wanting to use me; even while I was yet in my brokenness. I can't count the number of times women would come over to my house in Germany, and in the States, and cry their eyes out about their low self-esteem, self hatred, and not understanding their purpose, husbands and families. Suicide seemed to have been the answer for most of them if I would have let them. The spirit of suicide, anger, and depression was very strong in Germany around the Air Force base back in 1993-1997. The problem with this picture was I too was thinking the same thing. I would close my eyes as I would round steep curves on a two way mountain top road. I was hoping I would run off the road or get hit by a car. That way, in my little mind, I wasn't really committing suicide. Since I didn't really commit suicide, I might just get to heaven after all.

my past defined who I was

Some days I would act like the elephant man in front of my children and say, *"I am not an animal, I am a person,"* just to hear laugher in my home again. My spirit was screaming within myself saying; "I am a person, not a slave. I can think of brilliant ideas that can change lives. I too have the power and the authority to subdue the earth. So why am I letting myself be ruled by other people's opinions about who I am. I am not an animal to be controlled." What I was really trying to say was would **someone please define who I am.**

I was told so many times and I believed I was on my way to hell because I wouldn't forgive my husband, mother, father, and all the friends that had hurt me in my lifetime. My mind set was okay, let's get this party started. Life and hell was now intermixing. I didn't know where one began and where one ended. They became one and the same. I couldn't take the verbal abuse anymore. No matter what I did, I couldn't please my god (husband) anymore. Instead of being full of Christ and His anointing, I was full of my husband and his burdens. Even after returning from Germany all I believed in was failing apart right in front of my eyes. The past was repeating itself and marriage problems had shown up again. The core of what I thought made up a family, was now being tested day by day. I was questioning everything. What is the role of a husband and father? What was my role as a wife and mother and where did God fit into the picture? After returning state side, I told myself this and I lived by these words, When going back is not longer an option, I then can go forward out of my Egypt, the past."

It was the hand of my loving Father that brought me out of Germany. No one else could have done it like Him. Please don't get me wrong, Germany was not the problem. The place is very beautiful and the people were nice. The problem lay deep inside my mind and spirit. One can have an Egypt experience anywhere, where there is no peace of mind; Egypt is just around the corner waiting on you. The children of Isreal were physically out of Egypt, or their past, but their mindset kept them in their past. Everything around me favored my past and God sent an earthquake to knock me off the throne of my past. My whole world was **now** being challenged from this perspective. I kept praying the scripture Heb 12:27 and wanting God to shake the hell loose from my life. My Egypt or my past became my **now**. I did not want to go back to my past but it showed up everyday. I was living in the past.

Chapter 14

The Toilet Experience

One day I was sitting on my bed in my bedroom looking into my bathroom at the toilet.

God then asked me, "What is that?"

I thought for a moment and was very puzzled by the question.

I said, "It's a seat."

God responded, "Yes, it is. What else is it?"

I said, "It could be a throne."

He said, "Yes, what do you do with a throne?"

I replied, "I sit on it."

God then said, "Very good. What do you do when you sit on it?"

I said, "I allow things to pass from me."

The tears came from no where and filled my eyes. My spirit became overwhelmed from this effortless revelation from my Father, "I sit on the throne and allow things to pass." I had to say it over and over again to get the profoundness of the meaning of what God was trying to say to me. The significance of it extended far below the surface of my understanding. It hit my deep seated characteristics of bitterness and anger I was carrying around inside my spirit sense childhood. Then like the loving Father He is, He asked me "Do you allow things to pass? I had to say, "No, father, I do not."

God then said this, "Tangela I have never seen you reach back into the toilet after having a bowel movement and say, Lord please let me keep this chunk of waste. I still have need of it." At that time in my life, I didn't truly understand what **now** was. I slept in my past. I woke up in my past. I walked in the past. The past itself became my future. I became the perfect example of Proverbs 23:7 which says, *"For as he thinketh in his heart, so is he."* I continually gave birth to my past over and over again in my heart. My heart formed my words, and my words formed my world. Therefore, I became what I thought which was my *past*. I meditated on the lie brought to me by negative words, and I believed the lie over the truth. All of my decisions were based on my past hurts, failures, shames, and disappointments. I thought if I could keep them in the forefront of my mind, I wouldn't make the same mistakes again. Or even better, I wouldn't be like my parents but I was sadly mistaken. But all I accomplished with my efforts was building a wall of anger and fear around me and all my **issues.** I was keeping out my husband, children, loved ones, and friends. I kept them far away from me and my foul mouth. This left me alone to experience the cold rigid hands of isolation and loneliness; I was in a place that was full of darkness, pain and it had no light or life in it.

naked and ashamed

One day I turned to my husband with tears in my eyes and asked him, "Can you teach me how to dance with you again? I somehow lost the steps." What I was really trying to say to him was, "I'm so tried of dancing alone in this marriage. Can we dance together **now**?" There were more times than I care to mention that I wouldn't let my husband touch me. It seemed like every touch of his reminded me of a childhood touch of pleasure and then shame. How do you explain the feelings of abuse to your husband, but not having any memory of it? My days were spent hiding behind the mask of "Religiosity" and a false sense of righteousness. This is when you know there is a God, but you do not want to have a true relationship and intimacy with Him and His word. I did not want to be **naked** because I was **ashamed.** Adam or Tangela, where are you?

God would look at me spiritually, with my hands in the toilet, holding on to the defiled waste of my past. I was crying out, "Please don't make me let this go." God would say to me, "*Just flush and let the water wash it away from your life. It is no longer a part of you. It came to pass; not to stay for a* **lifetime**. *Why do you continue to hold on to the waste of yesterday's hurts?*" My response would be, "This piece right here, I'll keep it near my heart so that others won't harm me again. Lord, that other piece floating in the water, I'll take that one too because I don't trust you enough to take them. God you have let me down so many times. How can I trust you with my life **now**?" I would sit on the "Throne of The Past" and because I didn't trust God enough, I wouldn't let anything pass from me. I became spiritually constipated and was in need of a colon cleanse.

God then took me to His word over and over again. He was trying to get me to start my divine cleanse. In Hebrews 10:22 it says,

> *"Let us go right in, to God himself, with true hearts fully trusting him to receive us, because we have been sprinkled with Christ's blood to make us clean, and because our bodies have been washed with pure water," (The Way Bible). In Ephesians 5:26-27 it says, "That he might Sanctify and cleanse it with the washing of water by the word. That he might present it to himself a glorious church, not having spot, or wrinkle, or any such thing; but that it should be holy and without blemish."*

We tie the hands of God when we don't forgive or release our **past**. God can't take us **pass our past**. It is a choice we must make **now**. After, and only after, there is a **passing** away of the **past**, **God speaks**. Joshua had to be told the same thing in the bible. In Joshua 1:1-2, 5-8, the Way Bible says this:

> *"After the death of Moses, the Lord's disciple, God spoke to Moses' assistant, whose name was Joshua (the son of Nun), and said to him, "NOW" that my disciple is dead, (you are the new leader of Israel). Lead my people across the Jordan River into the Promised Land. I say to you what I said to Moses: No one will be able to oppose you as long as you live, for I will be with you just as I was with Moses; I will not abandon you or fail to help you. You need only to be strong and courageous and to obey to the letter every law Moses gave you, for if you are careful to obey every one of them*

you will be successful in everything you do. Constantly remind the people about these laws, and you yourself must think about them every day and every night so that you will be sure to obey all of them. For only then will you succeed."

God only gave His instructions to Joshua after the passing of Moses.

make a choice to live or stay in the past

Moses then represented God's testimony on the earth. God's history also gave Joshua a choice to go forth into the **now of God's presence**, or stay in the **past of Moses**. Before He told Joshua He would be with him, like he was with Moses all the days of his life, He waited on Joshua to make a choice in his spirit. God wanted to know if Joshua would trust God like Moses did and move into the movement of God for his time. God made a statement in Joshua 1:2, *"Moses my servant is dead; now therefore arise."* It was like God was telling him to get yourself together over the death of Moses. There is still more work that needs to be done **now,** not in the **past.** In other words, make a choice to live **now** in me or stay in the **past.** This was the question God kept on asking me. **"Make a choice, Tangela."** I made that choice and the day of my cleansing came and many more followed behind it. Remember, deliverance is a process, not an experience. Deliverance is something that takes time. I was ready to make a choice to leave the past behind.

God gave me my tears back and the cleansing started. Tears are words not spoken. They are the non-verbal rainfalls of the inner spirit of man created to cleanse the soul. But when it is all said and done, "The Passing of the Past makes one feel spotless inside and out." Each cleansing, I felt like Hezekiah Walker's song "Won't He make you clean inside!" My spiritual weights began to fall off me and miraculously, the physical weight followed. I am emerging into a beautiful butterfly. I have taken my choice, my power to change and put it back into the potter's hands. I said to God, "Transform me with the renewing of your word that I might live and not die."

Understanding Your Destiny

ebster's dictionary define **destiny** as: **to direct or set apart for a specific purpose or place; a predetermined course of events often held to an irresistible power.** We will be looking at these two definitions of **destiny.** The first part of the definition is found in Psalms 32:8. This talks about how God will instruct you, lead you, and be your help throughout your lifetime. It says, *"I will instruct you (says the Lord) and guide you along the best pathway for your life: I will advise you and watch your progress."* Your beginning existence, being, reality, and your way of life start with God who gave you your purpose, and destiny. Like any father, He wants to be the one who helps you throughout life. Since God gave you these gifts, purpose and destiny, why not ask Him how they should work **best** in your life. Remember God wants His best for you and He is the ultimate instructor of all life forms. What the Father wants to do is impregnate your mind with **His** knowledge of how to live. If we would only allow the Father to teach and train us on the way we should go, when we become mature, we will not forsake Him or His ways. When we follow **His** instructions, they will always lead us to the place called **now.**

The second part of the definition of **destiny** is **a predetermined course of events often held to an irresistible power.** These **events** are called **trials** and **tribulations.** What are trials and tribulations? Good question to ask. The simplest definition is they are life's every day problems, and the cares of this world that can cause us stress. Your second question might be what is God's purpose for using trials and tribulations in our lives? God uses them to teach us His knowledge and to build our faith in His ability to answer our prayers. In I Peter 1:7, the Way Bible states this, "*These trials are only to test your faith, to see whether or not it is strong and pure. It is being tested as fire tests gold and purifies it-and your faith is far more precious to God than mere gold; so if your faith remains strong after being tried in the test tube of fiery trials, it will bring you much praise and glory and honor on the day of his return.*" The Bible talks about tribulations and how God's children can over come those too. Tribulations simply means three times the trouble and they don't have to emotionally or physically drain us. In St John 16:33 it says, "*I have told you these things, so that in Me you may have [perfect] peace and confidence. In the world you have tribulation and trials and distress and frustration; but be of good cheer [take courage; be confident, certain, undaunted]! For I have overcome the world. [I have deprived it of power to harm you and have conquered it for you.]*" Trials and tribulations are the events in the process of life God uses to bring us into **now.**

You will never get to the future God has for you until you deal with your **now**. **Now** is based on your destiny or future and the process of life's trials and tribulations in your **past** you have **successfully** come through. Only then can one turn to another brother or sister and lend them a helping hand. A hand that is not full of criticism, condemnation, and disapproval but a hand that has been strengthened by God to reach those who have lost their way. The word successfully in this context means to take responsibility of ones actions and emotions. Then look at them for what they really are. Then assigning meaning to them, but leaving the negative elements of your actions and emotions behind you. Leaving you with the building blocks of a positive life style and not a negative one, a life-style people would like to see in their own lives. This is how we start to become a living testimony to the world around us. This positive life style can be accomplished only after the "BLAME GAME" has ended. This is truly taking the success out of life and applying it into our own. In St Luke 22:31-32 states this: "*And the Lord said, Simon, Simon, behold, Satan hath desired to have you, that he may sift you as* wheat: *But I have prayed for thee, that thy faith fail not: and when thou art converted, strengthen thy brethren.*" Remember God has brought us out of sin. To takes us into His light, so we can bring others out. This is the process of salvation: He brought us out, to take us in, to bring others out.

Your life was predetermined or foreordained and the Bible in Romans 8:28-32 proves that. You were appointed in advance when God's words of destiny were decreed and spoken over you. You're not an accident! You're not a product of rape because your origin began in God and it didn't start in an act of violence. Therefore your life is not *worthless* or *useless*.

You are **somebody** in spite of how you had to enter into your destiny and purpose. You're not a product of your mother forgetting to take her birth control pill. You were **not** created out of the forgetfulness of your mother. Your life is a well thought out plan that came from the God of Abraham. Man can't stop what God has blessed, ordained, and decreed to come forth. **SO YOU ARE SOMEBODY IN CHRIST!!** The Bible states this truth about God's integrity, character and nature. He is a God that never changes in these areas. God may change in the way he instructs His children throughout generations, but His nature will never be altered. Not even when God was in flesh. The Bible says this truth about our God. He can't lie and He will not change His mind like men do. *"God is not a man, that he should lie; He doesn't change his mind like humans do. Has He ever promised? Without doing what He said? Look! I have received a command to bless them, For God has blessed them, And I cannot reverse it,"(Numbers 23: 19-20 The Way Living Bible).* The most profound statement in this scripture is *"God is not a man."* God is the spirit of **truth** and there are no gray or shaded areas in God. When God decrees that you were blessed before the foundation of the earth was created, you are **blessed!!** No mother or father, spouse, teacher or boss can change you from being **blessed**. Nothing in heaven or hell can take that away from you, except you and your <u>choices.</u>

the wait is over

The next step in God's process was creating us an earth suit. In receiving ours bodies we also received dominion and authority on the earth. Our spirits without an earthly temple had no legal right or dominion on the earth. Once God made us a temple in His image we no longer live in the "*wait*" of God. The second God joined our spirits with our bodies, the wait was over. We move and have our being in His ***Now***. Yes, the bible says in Isaiah 40:31, "*But they that <u>wait</u> upon the Lord shall renew their strength; they shall mount up with wings as eagles; they shall run, and not be weary; and they shall walk and not faint.*" Our spirit waited on God to create us a physical body. After receiving our new bodies, the waiting was over for us. 1 Corinthians says "*But God gives it a body as He pleases, and to each seed its own body.*" The instant God created our bodies, He also finished His work in us by releasing purpose and destiny into our temples.

There is nothing more for God to do so we must follow the journey of our life to find our destiny. We must see where our journey leads us. I tell people this all the time, "Yes, God is the author and the finisher of our faith and no man or woman knows their ending. If we did know our ending, would we still want to walk life's pathway? What if we knew the precise time, day and year when all things would end for us? That's like God giving you a life sentence within your life. Instead of life being a journey full of wonders and surprises each day, it then becomes a walk of death every <u>now</u> of our lives. We would be walking in fear of what is to come and not in the measure of faith." Faith is trusting in God that we will see Him. Not only see Him at the end of our journey, but also in our everyday life. God is the starting place of our completion, and in Him we are completed.

Our God is a finisher. What He starts, He also finishes, "*Looking unto Jesus the author and finisher of our faith,*"*(Hebrews 12: 2)*. We have heard and read this scripture many times. But I just "**NOW**" got it. Why did the word of God refer to Jesus and not to the Father *alone* as the author and finisher of our faith? We all know it was God who created everything seen and unseen. But yet the bible said that Jesus is the author and the finisher of our faith. Why? In the bible it states this truth about Jesus; "*And the Word (Christ) became flesh (human, incarnate) and tabernacle (fixed His tent of flesh, lived awhile) among us; and we [actually] saw His glory (His honor, His majesty), such glory as an only begotten son receives from his father, full of grace (favor, loving-kindness) and truth,*"(*St. John 1:14 amplified bible*). To be an author, one must have written a book and Christ wrote our lives as a book.

our lives are a book of words

A book has words in it. Words then become the focus point in understanding the author and his purpose for writing and finishing the book. The author then picks words that would best portray his personality and characterize what they want to say. The author wants the reader to follow him very closely with each word that he chooses. The author's choice of words are based on the images they will produce in the readers mind. This gives the reader a clear picture on what the author is saying in the book. The main purpose for writing a book is to be able to tell *your story* from beginning to end.

Words are more than just putting together letters of the alphabet. They are energy. Words are sounds which create images that cause our bodies to react to them. A single spoken word can manifest life or death to the hearer or to the one who is giving the word. This is the powerful unseen force that is found in just one word. So, what does all of this have to do with **Jesus Christ.** He is not just the Father or our author and finisher of our faith. Why is Jesus and His anointing as equally important to us as the Father? We read earlier in this chapter (St. John 1:14) that Christ is the words that comes out of the Father's mouth. Christ is God's imagination in word form. Without God releasing His words, there wouldn't be an earth or man to live on or in it. It was God the Father releasing Christ the Son to create what the Father had seen in His mind. Jesus is the spoken word of God manifested in human form. There wouldn't be Jesus Christ without the Father. There wouldn't be an earth or people to live on the earth without Christ the Son of God. Christ is the spoken word of God *<u>released.</u>*

before a thought becomes a word

The word author also means creator. In Webster's dictionary, it defines author as: *originator; one that originates or gives existence: source; God*. The author's words then becomes his self expression to the readers. They are also the spoken vocabulary of his most inner thoughts and testimonies. Before a thought becomes a word, it is merely an image in the author's mind. With each image from a word, there is a different reaction that moves our body to respond to it. This is how powerful a single word is. God thought out and planned how He wanted the earth and man to look in his mind. He then commanded His words (Christ) to come forth out of the darkness of His imagination. God recreated what He saw in His mind by just speaking the words. God's imagination is the beginning platform for all life forms. He released Christ (words) with all of His authority, control and influences to manifest the plans of God. He was telling the word's images where to begin and end. God told them how to form and what the form was to become. God wants to see what He imagined in His mind come forth into the physical realm called earth.

We must have faith to manifest what His words have created. The Father and Son both have equal parts in our faith. Everything that God has said and will say will come from Jesus who is God's spokesman. Jesus words are filled with the Father's anointing. This anointing comes from the Father with the authority to empower us to complete all that God has ordained for us to do. This is one of the reasons why so many Christians make this statement. "It is no longer I that live, but the Christ (anointing) that lives in me." We speak this statement in trying times or in times of triumph. Christ is the *dunamis* power that gives us strength, ability, abundance, and virtue. The Christ side that now lives in us is the spiritual side that keeps us connected to our heavenly Father. It is His words working through us that continually keep us in God's presence and our name in the book of life. This is why Christ is our author. It was His words from God the Father that created humanity and all the earth. We carry His words and His anointing within us. He is the spoken or *rhema* and written or *logos* word of God. Jesus is also the *finisher* of our faith. The minute Jesus became flesh and walked among us, He began to show us how to operate the God side of man while living in the flesh.

When the man named Jesus died on the cross, He said this, *"After this, Jesus, knowing that all was now finished (ended), said in fulfillment of the scripture, I thirst. When Jesus had received the sour wine, He said, It is finished! And He bowed His head and gave up His spirit," (St. John 19:28, 30).* When the flesh of Jesus died, our faith was completed in its fullness. There was nothing left for the Son of God to do to restore man back to the Father. Jesus Christ on the cross represented *man's spirit* and *flesh* being tested and judged by the Father. The Christ side is the author's side of Jesus. Christ represents God's power to create man's spiritual life with His words. The finishing side of Jesus, the man, is representative of how we should live our life on the earth.

Christ didn't need a physical body while in heaven. A physical body only became a need when the Father sent Him to be a living example to mankind. Jesus, the man, is our perfect example of how flesh and spirit can co-habit together on the earth without needing to sin. So, Jesus is the finisher of our flesh. Christ is the author of our spirit. This is why the scripture states that Jesus is our author (spirit) and finisher (flesh) of our faith. Jesus and His anointing was God's sacrificial lamb to restore our relationship back to the Father. He alone has all spiritual and physical power in His hand. Jesus and His anointing is the spirit that is placed inside woman's wombs to bring forth life, destiny, and purpose to man.

Chapter 16

An image created from the mind of God

The womb of a woman is likened to Genesis 1:2. In Genesis, God was creating the physical not the spiritual. When God placed the seed or destiny of life into our mother's wombs, our physical bodies started to take form. The woman's womb was **not** created by God to reproduce man's spirit, only the flesh of man. God didn't give man or woman the ability to create another man's spirit. God alone is the giver of spirit and life. Man's spirit is only created and released by God and not man. Remember man cannot choose his birthday. God was creating the physical, not the spiritual, in the first chapter of Genesis. In other words, God was forming the physical according to His imagination. The world then became God's interpretation of Himself. We are a physical manifestation of the image in the mind of God. The light, water, grass, day, night, stars, fish, fowls, and cattle were all manifestations in the physical realm (Gen 1: 2-11).

CHAPTER SIXTEEN

In the first Chapter of Genesis, God released the spirit of words to manifest the physical. God's words went from spiritual form to a physical form that He could see on the earth. The statement that God kept repeating *"Let there be"* simply means come forth in the *present* or the **Now**. God was commanding Himself to bring forth all that He was thinking in His mind or Imagination. Only God can command Himself to bring forth that which is of Him, the NOW and the Present.

In Genesis chapter 1:26-27 is the birthing of man's body out of God's spiritual womb, *"And God said, Let us make man in our image, after our likeness. Vs27 So God created man in his own image, in the image of God created he him; male and female created he them."* This scripture makes it very clear how God created man. In Genesis 1: 27, God speaks about the making of man three times. Here is the first time it is mentioned, *"So God created man in his own image…."* The Father was referring to the spirit of man. Man's spirit at this point during creation had no gender. Man's spirit represented mankind as a whole. So we are all created in the image of God.

God mentions the creation of man a second time in this same verse, *"in the image of God created He **him**."* The *he* represents God, who is the creator of all things. The *him* is singular this time. This refers to man's spirit receiving the power of choice from God to speak life and death. The third time creation is mentioned, it is in a third form,… *"male and female created He **them.**"* This was the first mention of man's spirit having two bodies, *male* and *fe-male*. God was making a distinction between man's spirit in two bodies. With each body, came different functions and similarities to God and then to each other. The scripture made this very clear when it said, *"male and female created He **them**."* We have the same spirit from God's image but different bodies with different functions.

Man's spirit went from one entity to form two separated bodies. Mankind now went from the singular form of man's spirit to the plural of two bodies, *male* and *female*. God then spoke this truth to me at my job one day, *"What God does in darkness will take man a lifetime to discover."* The spiritual womb of God is full of purpose and destiny for mankind. God's womb **is** existence, substance, reality, and a way of life. His womb has the ability to give life at will. The bible put it in these words so we can understand some dimension of His life giving womb, *"But as it is written, Eyes hath not seen, nor ear heard, neither have entered into the heart of man, the things which God hath prepared for them that love him. But God hath revealed them unto us by his Spirit: for the Spirit searcheth all things, yea, the deep things of God, "* (1 Corinthians 2:9-10). God knew what He was doing when he asked the trinity to make man spirit and body.

When God said, *"Let us make man in our image,"* He was talking to the trinity; Father, Son, and Holy Spirit. It took the trinity to complete the creation of man's spirit and body. It was like the Father saying, *"I will create the spirit of man"*. The Son of God then stated, *"I will give him my ability to speak the Father's word with power and might."* The Holy Spirit went on to say, *"I will be their teacher and comforter. I will teach the male and female the right choices on how to manifest change with the Father's words on the earth."* It was truly, let US make man in OUR image.

inside a woman's womb

The destiny of *man's spirit* was to become male and female. Our spirit was without physical form and we were void, which means not occupied;

vacant; not inhabited. Darkness was inside our mothers' womb. The Spirit of God, who gives life, moves inside the waters of our mothers' womb and brought forth God's images. When our bodies came forth from our mother's womb, they came out with the spirit of life, destiny and purpose. We were coming forth out of the darkness from one dimension to be birthed into another one. The first dimension is where God joins together the spirit of man to his flesh as one entity. This union gave man the ability to speak and walk with the same authority the Father has in heaven. Just like the Father, Son and Holy Spirit is also one, God wanted man's spirit and flesh to work together unity.

In man's life, the missing person or the void is the Father. God created a place in man's spirit, not his body, for Him to be invited into. When we invite God into our second dimension call *physical life,* we also invite a new *now.* This **NOW** was a physical dimension we grew to understand as our lifetime. Genesis 1:2 is the womb of God being opened. Whenever a womb is opened, the first two elements that come out are water and blood. This birth allowed the physical to come forth out of that which was eternal. In Jeremiah 33:2, it states, *"Thus saith the Lord the maker thereof , the Lord that formed it, to establish it; the Lord is his name."* What God has formed, He will also establish, complete, and finish. Before something is established, it must first be formed, thought out or planned in the mind. Then later it is birthed into physical form. Life and death are the beginning and the ending power of God. Before there can be a beginning, there must first be a *thought or a plan* of how to transcend the spiritual to physical form. God then asked me this question, *"Tangela what is greater than a beginning?"* Since God is the beginning of everything, I thought for a minute and asked myself what could be greater or equal to God? In the beginning was God. I couldn't come up with anything that is greater than God or the beginning? So I turned to my father and said I don't know. God replied *"A thought."* A thought is greater than a beginning or ending. Life nor death can happen until there is a beginning or thought. God is the alpha and the omega of all life forms. God is the only one who can birth life and death simultaneously.

When a new born enters into this world, death also enters into the child's life because of Sin. What looks like a beginning to us, is only the beginning of the end for the child. God creates and concludes the matter of ones life in a mere second of conception. In conception, God begins life and then concludes it. This is all done in the secret places of God that is found inside a woman's womb. A woman's womb is the life giving covering to protect the next generation and all of God's promises. It is the beginning of change and the ending of life for the nations. What comes forth out of her womb can strengthen a world or weaken it to its knees. Man's spirit and his destiny are linked together by God.

your spirit came directly from God

Destiny was a place inside man's spirit, not inside his body. Man's body can not contain the purpose that is produced from destiny. Man's body was made out of the dust of the earth and man's body will return back to it's original form, dust. But his spirit came directly from God and was full of His likeness and power to speak change. If destiny was placed inside of man's body, when he dies, his destiny would die too. Everything he has ever done would stop at the time of his death. Our heavenly Father wouldn't have anything to judge man with. Destiny and purpose needs a physical body to operate in a physical world. We then become our Father's hands and feet to get His will accomplished on the earth. His will is our life. His purpose is our destiny.

God doesn't have to ask man or woman to bring destiny or purpose to life. You were born with God's purpose and destiny, not man's. This is why at first, women are not always aware of the fact God has made choices that will bring about change in her life. Women do not fully understand that a newborn will come forth out of her belly filled with the rivers of life from God, *Out of his* (her) *belly shall flow rivers of living water,"* John 7:38. Yes, the children that burst forth from the woman's womb are the rivers that God is talking about. We were conceived and concealed in the water of life from God. It is God's water that sustains us through each trimester of life. When God releases us from the womb of a woman, water and blood came forth too. We must use the water of life to baptize our body, but it will take the blood of Jesus to cover our sin. If we choose to want to live again in Christ, we will wash ourselves in His blood. This washing of our spirit is a form of death.

Once the spirit and the body come together, death is also present. Our days are being numbered from the birthing of life, to death. Even in death, our spirits shall live on according to the book of Revelation. It will be your choice where_you choose to live in eternity. The minute our spirits are connected with our bodies, the waiting is over. We begin the race of life towards death.

It is like a runner who is at the starting blocks of a race. He is anticipating the sound of the gun going off. Then you hear those words that will let you know the race is about to begin. *"Runners take your mark.* The head is out of the womb. *"Get set."* The shoulders then follows, *"Go!"* The baby has entered into the world, now **BE** about your Father's business. God created us to "BE" in the "NOW" to finish the work He has started in the earth. He needs our hands to complete the cultivating of humanity and the earth. This "BE" means to be in the present of life, not in the past with your words or someone else's. It was God's destiny for you to BE on earth NOW to **renew** the purpose of God in mankind.

change and exchange

Let also look a little closer at the word *"renew"*. Isaiah 40:31 says, *"But they that wait upon the Lord, shall renew their strength."* The word **renew** has two separate but conjoined meanings in this passage. It means to **change** and **exchange** all at the same time. What are some of the things we have inside us that we need to have renewed or changed daily? If we are honest, we have a lot of things we would like to see **renewed** or **changed** about ourselves. Because of the fall of man into sin, our spirit is continually being attacked. We are like sheep being spiritually slaughtered daily, *"As it is written, For thy sake we are killed all the day long; we are accounted as sheep for the slaughter,"* Romans 8:36. Also, *"I affirm, by the boasting in you which I have in Christ Jesus our Lord, I die daily,"* I Corinthians 15:31. Our bodies are constantly changing from the time we were formed in our mother's womb, until our death. Paul explained this transformation in 1 Corinthians 13:11 which says, *"When I was a child, I spoke as a child, I understood as a child, I thought as a child; but when I became a man, I put away childish things."* We must change or renew our lives daily in wisdom, knowledge, and in experiencing His love.

The renewing or changing is God reminding us of our destiny in Him. Each day or **NOW** should remind us that God keeps His promises and His word, even if we don't keep ours. From our past to our future destiny, life should be based on our ability to understand how much God loves us. We were created by love and to be loved by Him.....NOW. Being renewed is leaving our past behind. It's leaving all the broken and fragmented pieces of our emotional and mental state behind us. Being renewed is a key part of the process of coming into the NOW of your life.

exchange our negative words

The word *renew* also means to **exchange**. We give up something in order to receive something. What are we exchanging on a daily basis with God? Are we exchanging our past words for a new life in Him? We must exchange words full of power to change us into what He has already ordained in the beginning. Negative words are our past that we carry with us throughout life. Negative words can control or even restrict our movements mentally or physically. They can be the cause of sickness in our bodies, mind and spirit. If we choose to hold on to negative words from our past, mental problems can develop later in our lives. Negative words from our past can stop us from applying for a new job, starting a new career in an unfamiliar place or state, going back to school to finish a degree, or even returning back to God. God wants us to exchange our negative words for his words.

God wants to exchange **our** words that don't say what He has said about us. He wants to **exchange** them for His words that will only bring joy and a peace of mind. We speak negative things about ourselves that God has not and is not saying about us. We look at the past of our lives and speak about the former things and forget the NOW. It is the NOW things in our life that help us reach our destiny.

God wants to take the former things of your life and exchange them for the NOW things of God, His promises. Please remember this thought that God told me, *"God might bring you to a familiar place, but never to your PAST."* God might have you to re-visit something that happened to you that caused great pain and anguish in your life. But He will never tell you to pick it up again and carry it. Nor will He want you to live in those tormenting memories once again. God wants you to **exchange** those thoughts of anger and resentment for His. Our God is a mender of broken vessels and spirits. He is just waiting on you to give it to Him. God's timing to activate His promises is based on your willingness to release.

Your spirit was in heaven, meaning eternity, waiting on the timing of GOD to activate purpose in you. This is why it was necessary for your father and mother to be in on the blessing. Man's spirit needed an earthly body to reproduce GOD'S glory in a physical world. Conception was only the beginning of your body and not your spirit and this is why we call it a **birthday**. It was God's designated day of birthing one's physical body, flesh, out of eternity and into **time** or earth. We were born into death. From the moment of physical conception in our mother's womb, our days were numbered here on this earth. This means we were born into a dying world because of sin. In Ecclesiastes 7:1-4, The Way Bible says, *"The day one dies is better than the day he is born! It is better to spend your time at funerals than at festivals. For you are going to die and it is a good thing to think about it while there is still time. Sorrow is better than laughter, for sadness has a refining influence on us. Yes, a wise man thinks much of death, while the fool thinks only of having a good time now."* I read some where on an e-mail this truth about life, *"Don't take life too serious; no one gets out alive."* We were born into this physical world to die.

Chapter 17

Feeling like Dorothy
...lost in the land of OZ

W e must take our NOW and find our purpose in it. In finding our purpose, our generation will find God's glory in our life and in our death. God alone has the power to give life or take it. We must honor and respect our heavenly Father for the true God He is. Our life started with God and it shall end with God, whether we acknowledge Him or not. Our decision to acknowledge Him does not diminish or deplete who He is. Acknowledging the creator in your everyday life is like Dorothy in the Wizard of OZ. In order for her to find her way back home, she had to come to grips and be aware of her NOW. She asked everyone that was around her where she was. Why? Because the NOW she experienced left her in a state of panic and confusion. Dorothy's life was in disarray and she didn't really understand how she got there. Her NOW, being in the land of OZ, left her in a state of shock. Her house was thrown from one end of the earth to another. Dorothy's life left her asking a lot of questions.

Dorothy went from understanding her environment to not accepting her NOW in a new and strange place. Her life was in total madness. All the old and familiar people and places were completely gone from her sight. The only thing she had left from her past was her dog ToTo and a memory of what used to be. When she awakened, she was in a new place in *time*. She needed to get a better insight on where she was **NOW**. Not the place she came from, but her **NOW**. Where are you NOW in life?

In this movie, Dorothy didn't fully appreciate the people who loved and care for her. She thought her loved ones didn't make enough time for her, so she decides to run away from what was familiar to her. She decided to go in search of an unknown reality that she had created in her mind. Dorothy's past *now's* with her loved ones were not fulfilling her personal needs at that time. How many times have life experiences left you spiritually bankrupt with no deposit for you or anyone else to withdraw from. She needed help from those that were around her to better understand where she was and how she got there. We too are like Dorothy and we need people to rally around us. If a NOW comes and causes disorder in our lives, we can only hope our loved ones will be there to assist us in the clean up. But we must see the disorder in our lives as part of the process of getting us to our destiny.

Dorothy also needed to recognize her Destiny. Her getting back home was the conclusion of the movie. But the land of OZ was the journey she needed to find her Destiny. She needed the land of OZ to experience and appreciate her NOW, her family and all the other people who cared and loved her so much. Sometimes we work so hard to get to where we are, we miss our NOWS of a lifetime. Once a NOW is over, you will never get it back. So don't just stop and smell the roses Dorothy, but celebrate that you did.

Dorothy also needed to know where she was going. Dorothy wanted to get back home to the place where her journey started. Remember, NOW is stepping out of one reality in to another. Dorothy experienced this when she woke up and found herself in the land of OZ. It was a brand new reality for her to deal with and an opportunity to face all the new challenges that comes with not knowing. In the book called "Understanding The Dreams You Dream" by Ira Milligan states, *"Storms are disturbances: Change; spiritual warfare; judgment; sudden calamity or destruction; persecution; opposition; witchcraft."* The scripture that he used to support his findings was this, *"The Lord hath His way in the whirlwind and in the storm, and the clouds are the dust of His feet, (Nahum 1:3b).* One moment you're married and thinking things are pretty good, even though your relationship is not that great. Yes, we have problems like everyone else, but nothing that can't be fixed, right? Then your reality is changed by one word, **divorce**, **cancer** or **death.** Then you find yourself like Dorothy did, in your home with a tornado from hell.

find the nearest yellow brick road back to your heavenly father

When the true storms of life come, it tears up everything you tried so hard to build. It leaves you holding on to a memory of what used to be your life. One NOW can change our reality for a lifetime. You will find yourself asking this question, "**HOW or WHAT AM I SUPPOSE TO DO**?" Here is your answer. You're to find the nearest yellow brick road and follow it back to your heavenly Father as fast as you can. Yes, there are people waiting in the midst of your turmoil and chaos to help you along the way. Help you, not carry you. You cannot change the past but you can make a choice in the NOW.

Dorothy first had to make a choice to move past the hurt, pain, and anger of loosing everything. Death came and took that person or persons. But it can't come back and get those same people again. This is a NOW that came and went in your reality. But it is over and a new **NOW** awaits you. The NOW asks her the question, "Will you recognize me as a new beginning of the rest of your life?" Dorothy made the choice to move forward and God had people waiting there to help her along the way. Don't worry, Dorothy didn't see her help at first neither. These people might seem small and insignificant in your life at first. But in their mouth holds the very words and directions you need to find your way to a new "NOW." God uses people and angels on the earth to get help to us. Let go of your pride and stop trying to hide from the very assistance you're asking God for.

Ask God where are these helpers? He will show you. You will be very surprised just like I was because they have been there all along. God said "<u>**He will never leave you or forsake you**</u>." That means NOW go find your true friends. In finding them, you will also find God's love and help that He left on earth for you. In their hands, you will find the hands of God. They will be full of all the things you will need to heal. Why do you think Dorothy and the prodigal son came back home? When our reality is challenged, our perspective, principles and standards about that reality is also being challenged, what we thought was right in our eyes is NOW wrong. What God was trying to show us all along, we can NOW see clearly.

just…… "be"

Our eyes are no longer tainted with what we wanted to see. We surrender to the new reality of this NOW, bad or good. You must know this is just the beginning and not the ending of life, no matter how bad it may seem. If you are still breathing, there is still time for faith and hope. If you don't have enough faith or hope, God will be more than happy to share some of His. NOW makes you look at where you are and helps you to better understand where you need to **BE. BE** in the *present* where you can find your way back to the Father.

Now that you have found your way back to the presence of your Father, new life can began. Your new life is only going to be found in the presence of healing, understanding, forgiveness, and God's love. The problem that most people have is they don't understand their BE. Bishop Eddie Long said it like this, *"Just "BE" all that God has created you to "BE"*. We need to stop trying to BE and start living the BE of God's purpose in our life. The Army understands this very well. They have a campaign slogan that said, *"Be all you can be in the Army."* If the Army gets it, why is it so hard for the Army of the Lord to get these same very important principles? People, just relax and BE about the Father's business in the earth.

Let's BE fruitful and multiply. Let's subdue the earth using all its vast resources so the earth can service God and man. Let's have dominion over everything that creeps on the ground or is in the sea. That also means stop polluting our fresh waters and sea waters. This was man's original "NOW" that came from the Creator of life. Our "NOWS" have purpose, wisdom, and knowledge packed into it. **Now** is God's instructional manual on how to live and care for the earth. God can only become or reveal to you what you are willing to yield to Him. Your yielding will produce His revealing of Himself to you. Dorothy's first response was like so many of us who are trying to work it out and then ask questions later. But the minute Dorothy yielded herself to the NOW reality (Land of OZ) and stopped trying to do things her way, God revealed to her the *power* within herself all along to get back home.

Chapter 18

Lost in a maze called life

When God created you, He put all the necessary elements you will ever need to find your way back to the Father. He really meant it when He said, *"It is finished."* You are complete and lacking nothing but the faith to realize it. Dorothy didn't even know she had such power down inside her until one day a tornado or storm came by to put pressure on her to release her hidden power and find her way back home. The power of God's likeness is in us to help us move from one NOW to another, just like Dorothy did. Please keep this in mind: Not knowing where you are can be hazardous to your health. You can get lost physically if you don't know where you are going. All you need to do is to make a wrong turn while traveling. But that lost person is only in a temperary situation. The person who is spiritually lost, doesn't know where their NOW is. That person is lost in a maze called life and trying to find their way out quick and in a hurry. There is a way out of the maze.

Our spirit came from God and it is looking for ways to return back unto the Father. Remember God is our beginning and He is our ending too. Matthew 10:28 says, "*And fear not them which kill the body, but are not able to kill the soul; but rather fear him which is able to destroy both soul and body in hell.*" Your lifetime is the result of God blowing His breath into your body (Job 33:4). This is why we can speak to life in the power and the authority that Jesus' name gives us. Out of life we can call forth understanding of our purpose and destiny that our father created before the foundation of this world, (Jeremiah 1:5). We were given this authority over our life as a child of GOD. I dictate to life, life doesn't dictate to me!! Life then becomes the lifetime I need for my God given purposes to be established and to reproduce my Father's glory here on the earth. Ecclesiastes 6:10-11 says it this way, "*All things are decided by fate; it was known long ago what each man would be. So there's no use arguing with God about your destiny. The more words you speak, the less they mean, so why bother to speak at all? (The Way Living Bible)*

it's time to respond to your ability

This is our responsibility, to respond to the ability that God has given us as Christians. As Christians, we must take this responsibility very serious and get back on our knees. We must pray to our Father to intervene on our behalf to make Godly changes in ourselves and in this world. Our *destiny* will not be fully understood until we understand why the creator released our spirit to this earth. True Destiny in its basic form is to return back to the Father with His assignment for our lives completed and in hand, leaving behind all our excuses. It's time to deal with your past so you can reach your destiny.

The past and the future, or your destiny, are two Great forces. The past and future colliding together, produces movement, trembling, upheaval, and radical change. The purpose of the earthquake, caused by the faults in your life is the change of your **next decision**, which will lead you to your NOW. God won't let you go any further until you deal with your NOW, not your past, not your future, but your **NOW**. In Hebrews 12:27 it says, "*And this word, yet once more, signifieth the removing of those things that are shaken, as of things that are made.*" God is shaking our very foundation and challenging our decision making skills. God wants us to know "why are we making the choices that we make?"

Chapter 19

I only have the power
to change me

God started with my sick concepts of who I thought I was. Then, He taught me the value of self worth through His word. I started journaling back in 1993, but this time it took a different perceptive. Each time I would write about my husband and start complaining about him, God would stop me right in the middle of it and ask me this question, "Who in this marriage do you have the power to change?" But no matter what I would say to God, He would ask me the same question again and again until it was deeply implanted into my spirit. God kept telling me to make this statement, "I only have the power to change me." I would say it over and over again. Each time I would want to change my husband, children, family, church members, and co-workers attitudes, God would make me say, "I only have the power to change me."

I began to finally get His understanding. It is not my responsibility to change anyone in my household, at work or even in the world. **Change must start with me**. It is my responsibility as a parent to show, to train, and to be an example of how to live a Godly lifestyle. By doing that, others will see the Christ in me and ask me what is the difference. But I had to start change with me first. I heard someone say this in church one Sunday morning, "Where ever I go, I do ministry….. I only use words when necessary." What a powerful statement to say. It is not all about what you say because your actions will always overtake your words; just ask your children. It's not as much about what you say as it is what you do. I was saying I had to change, but I needed to do something NOW.

I heard my Father's words say this,

> *"NOW Tangela let's start with you. If I have only empowered you to change you, then stop bringing up other people. How can you tell me you love me, when you don't love yourself? I made you in my image and you have my likeness running through your veins."*

God's love letters to me, meaning the bible, said it this way,

> *"You made all the delicate, inner parts of my body and knit them together in my mother's womb. Thank you for making me so wonderfully complex! It is amazing to think about. Your workmanship is marvelous-and how well I know it. You were there while I was being formed in utter seclusion! You saw me before I was born and scheduled each day of my life before I began to*

breathe. Every day was recorded in your book! How precious it is, Lord to realize that you are thinking about me constantly! I can't even count how many times a day your thoughts turn towards me. And when I awakened in the morning, you are still thinking of me, (Psalms 139:13-18 The Way Living Bible).

These were God's words lavishing me with His love. I didn't know that my Father cared so much about **me**. Believe me, He feels that way about you too. Yes, YOU! His love letters continued about me in Psalms 8:5-6, "*….and yet you have made him only a little lower than the angels, and placed a crown of glory and honor upon his head. You have put him in charge of everything you made; everything is put under his authority,*" (*The Way Living Bible*). Yes, God has made man a little lower then Himself and put all things under his authority because that's how much God loves us.

discovering the power of a single word

The bible is full of all these love letters from God. Letters telling His children just how important we are to Him. I began to read His word as if He was writing to me personally. It was as if I was hearing them for the first time. His words became medicine to me. They nurtured the most inner parts of my soul. I **NOW** realized that I couldn't see my *now*, because I was blinded by my pain. His words became a song of love that fed my spirit. I could feel His breath as I exhaled the darkness of my life. I began to inhale the love of my Father. Hope began to enter back into the shell of the person

I was. My soul and spirit opened the under belly of my wounds. I began allowing the words of God to make love to me again. It was so beautiful to feel the Father's love filling up my emptiness. It was as if His words became spirits with wings on them, and they flew into my inner space, called understanding. The emptiness that was inside of me, began to hold on to every word my Father spoke. The memory of life was as if school was **NOW** in session.

I started like a child in preschool, with all the wonder and surprise of **a word**. I started trying to   understand the world of words again. I was curious as to how a word might be able to open up my closed life again. I began to understand the value of a WORD, not a chapter, not a paragraph, not even a sentence, just one single WORD at a time. I realized what I needed most was to hear <u>a word</u> from my heavenly father to began life over. My spirit was in desperate need of my Father's proceeding word. I needed His creative word. The same words He spoke that begin all life forms in heaven and on the earth. The words God begin to speak started my *change of life*. Remember, *change* is a *thought* manifested and then acted upon. I was being reborn. Each new word from God opened my understanding of who I was. I was discovering who God was and He was telling me who I was.

I chose to listen to God. Discovering God in the NOW of your life is the beginning of your destiny, and the ending of reliving your past over and over again. **If you want to know how to stop the cycle of pain in your life and stop reliving the memory of pain, start exchanging your past hurts and pains with your Father's love.** Let Him speak life into you with his words. But you must chose to hear God because the father has not stopped speaking. It is all about **choices** we make every day, every minute, and every second of our lives. Staying in the NOW of your life is based on the choices you choose to make in those moments. That's right, every moment. Start with the next moment in your life. You must ask yourself this question, **"When is enough, enough?"** At the end of this question, you will find the answer to the **NOW** of your change.

after understanding a word

I found out principles, powers, and the authorizations I had in His words. The more I read with understanding, the more I wanted to know what my Father had for me. What was waiting for me was His promises He made through his covenant with Jesus. I accepted Jesus into my life but NOW I knew God intimately. I was becoming even more and more aware of my inheritance and the right to have what was mine. I was told over and over again what a woman couldn't do or be in the church or in society. That was not enough for me. I went to the Father because I needed to know what He had for Tangela. When I attempted to validate what I was told about women in the bible, I couldn't find it. But what I did find was women in the bible who were pastors and ministers and so much more. I realized then that God liberated the woman when He took her out of man's temple and made her one of her very own. So this meant a woman had the same promises and authority as the man.

Women, female, no longer solely or exclusively relied only on the man to hear what God was saying to her. She too could approach the throne of God.

A woman could ask her heavenly Father what was on her heart without the help of man. God made the woman an independent person relying on God for her spiritual *substance*. She is to be in partnership with man to subdue and have authority over the earth. Suddenly, I was discovering a new life. I was discovering what a woman was to God.

true submission

Yes, the woman is to be submissive to her husband. Submission in marriage is a given because *God* stated that the man is the head or the governing leader. But I also saw that everyone needed to be in submission to someone. So I needed to know what and who I needed to submit to. What I NOW need to know was God's interpretation of the word *submissiveness*. I looked up the word in the dictionary to get a better understanding of the atmosphere or the content of the meaning of submissiveness.

I thought submissiveness was all about being less than a man because I was taught to believe this was God's way for women to live their lives. Where did I get such an off balance perspective in my life? This off balanced perspective that I had about what I thought was *submissiveness*, started in my parent's home. My mother was the head and still is the head of her home. I do not have a problem with women being strong leaders in their homes. It becomes a problem when one's leadership over powers or dominates the other person and their opinion. I saw and lived with this type of behavior until I left my mother's house. I grew up looking for a man who would be the opposite of my father and I found him. But the opposite of off balance is still **off balance.** If God is not the center of any relationship, then that relationship will be off balanced. My off balanced perspective about submissiveness didn't stop there.

After getting married and listening to the pulpits, society, and TV, they continued to distort my already distorted way of thinking. This distorted view lead me to believe I was somehow less than a man because of the vagina God gave to me. Eve sinned and somehow that made all the women subservient to every man on the earth. I now know that this is a lie from hell to distort or misrepresent the woman's spirit and position. I needed to get a better understanding to move forward into my NOW. Once I received the **true** understanding of submission from the bible, I can reclaim my power and my position. I ran to find the nearest dictionary. While I was looking up the word, I was asking the Holy Spirit to please give me the understanding I so desperately needed. I needed to find my purpose, position, and function in this life as a woman, mother and a wife. I know in God's words, the right understanding makes all the difference.

I didn't know the author of life

My spirit was crying out loud and thirsting for *His* understanding. In the bible, it states this, *"But there is [a vital force] a spirit [of intelligence] in man, and the breath of the almighty gives men understanding" (Job 32:8).* In Proverbs 2:6 it states this truth, *"For the Lord gives skillful and godly wisdom; from His mouth come knowledge and understanding."* Man's understanding can be rooted and grounded in tradition. I asked God what is tradition to Him. My Father replied with this statement, "*The experience or the mundane occurrence of life without God…….. It becomes null and void; it is the practice of life without purpose.*" I was willingly choosing man's words over God to define my purpose and function on the earth. Why? I didn't know the author of life!! I was submitting my life more to man than to God. It was the tradition!

My husband's words and actions were defining me and not God. Instead of being filled with the Holy Spirit who is the teacher of all things, I was filled with *my* spirit, *my parent's* spirit and *my husband's*. They were all just a misinterpretation of what a woman, mother, and a wife should be. I was allowing the teaching of man's tradition to dictate what *they thought* the word *submission* meant. Their teaching shaped and molded my life to what *their* expectations were and not God's. This left my life void and empty and canceled out everything God was showing me about me. What God was showing me in His word was so very different from man's traditions. I was discovering who I was and I wanted to learn more.

God has created women with more helpfulness than just being a neck or short skirt that can turn a head. We can make business decisions and own those same businesses. Women can and do have a career and maintain a home, sometimes with the help of the man. The man who helps this kind of woman is a man who understands who he is. A real man is not threatened by a woman who is making the necessary decisions while performing her purpose. I decided then, I will no longer try to manipulate my husband or degrade my position as a woman and a helpmate just to get what I need. I will simply turn and ask for what is RIGHT in the sight of God without the attitudes of insecurity. This is what the virtuous woman did in Proverbs 12:4.

The virtuous women was a secure woman who knew how to step to her God, to man, and to society to ask for what was her God given rights, *"A Virtuous woman is a crown to her husband: but she that maketh ashamed is as rottenness in his bones."* Married women are their husband's glory and we need to **BE** that. Stop asking for permission to **BE** the woman God has created you to **BE**. In the bible, Proverbs 31:10 continues to talk about the virtuous woman,

> *"If you can find a truly good wife, she is worth more that precious gems! Her husband can trust her, and she will richly satisfy his needs. She will not hinder him, but help him all her life. She finds wool and flax and busily spins it. She buys imported food, brought by ship from distant ports. She gets up before dawn to prepare breakfast for her household, and plans the day's work for her servant girls. She goes out to inspect a field, and buys it; with her own hand she plants a vineyard. She is energetic, a hard worker, and watches for bargains. She works far into the night!*

Ladies, did you hear what the word of God is saying to you. If you and your husband have already discussed and came into agreement about buying land or anything else, then do it. What if it is the wrong decision? Then learn from it and try not to make the same mistake twice and please don't criticize each other for making wrong decisions. Ladies, I have learned we have power, intuition, and discernment beyond our own understanding. These valuable and priceless tools God placed inside of a woman are there so man or woman can bring them out at will. The bible makes this statement about these qualities God hid inside of a woman, "*He who finds a [true] wife finds a good thing and obtains favor from the Lord,*" *(Proverbs 18:22 KJV AMPLIFIED.)* He called these traits hidden inside a woman His *favor*. This is one of the many ways for man and mankind to obtain God's favor in their lives. These characteristics are what our husbands, our businesses and the work force needs in order for them to be successful in the business world. Women use your Godly intuition and make change happen for you and those around you. When a woman understands her position, she also understands her unrestricted power from God. This means no man or woman can stop her from achieving her purpose. The virtuous women knew her position and her power. So ladies, let go of your past and let *change* happen NOW.

The virtuous woman didn't degrade any part of her womanhood, purpose, or destiny. So why do we think we need to do this today? Our function is to be a helpmate and mother of God's inheritance called children. But our purpose and destiny is the ministry God has put inside us. He created you for a specific purpose and it should bless you and help others in the process. It is also the head's job to cover and cultivate that gift. Someone should be covering you while you walk towards your destiny. He should not only do this for his wife and children but the proceeding ministry that comes out of his helpmate and children. It's a team or family effort to help everyone reach their God ordained destiny. Make a decision NOW! You have the Power of NOW in your life but you must use it to BE.

Chapter 20

It's your time to make love with the father

The quality of any relationship is determined on how each person meets the need of the other person in the relationship. If you feel like I felt, you really need the Father right now. You need someone to hold and caress you. You need some intimacy with no strings attached. Intimacy can only happen when words find trust in the innermost places of the heart. Communicating it is not all about you and what you want. If this kind of communication is going on in your marriage, home, work, or with family members, it is off balance and God is not pleased. Intimacy is about meeting each others needs and the Father wants to be intimate with you. The intimacy you need will only come from the father. It's time to make love with the father.

God began to explain what the act of love making was for. He said this to me, "*Love making is the place where man, woman and God's love meets as one*".

Man enters into the gates of heaven, the woman's vagina, and there is an explosion of pleasure and a river of life waiting for the two to become one in the presence of our Father. It's reconfirming each others love and God's covenant of marriage each time this beautiful act is performed. Where else on earth can three persons become one? Love making is actually God, man, and woman becoming one. Only God could create such a beautiful harmony that would represent His trinity here on the earth. We are truly made in His likeness. It is the ultimate ballet of love, the spirit of God and His word manifesting in man's body as one. At that very moment of ecstasy, we mere mortals are raptured up into our Father's love. For only mere seconds, our spirit is taken to the throne of God to experience all His love He has for us at once. Think about this for a moment. If an orgasm were to last any longer than seconds, we would pass out from His expression of love. God wants to be intimate with you NOW; this is how he will bring about change.

make a choice in who you will serve "NOW"

There are two great forces colliding together, which produces movement, trembling, upheaval, radical change, and the transforming of your **Next Decision**. One is called the your **PAST** and the other is called your **FURTURE** which leads you to "NOW." NOW is a place in time. Your Father, God, won't let you go any further until you deal with your NOW!! Not deal with your past, not your future, but your NOW. Your PAST trials and tribulations were instrumental in the process of life to get you to this place called NOW. You will never get to the future God has for you until NOW is dealt with. A decision in NOW is an open door to your future. The bible puts it in these words, "And if it seem evil unto you to serve the Lord, choose you **this day** (NOW) whom ye will serve; But as for me and my family, we will serve the Lord,"(Joshua 24:15 King James). What this scripture in saying is *make a choice in who you will serve "NOW".* Will you continue to serve your past? Will you keep viewing its painful memories as if it is a movie in your mind that never ends? Will you keep serving this movie of your past that keeps showing your mistakes and past failures every minute and second of each day of your life? God is asking you to choose the NOW that He has created for you and be persistent, relentless, and determined to choose NOW over your past each time it makes its way to your mind.

Keep telling yourself,

"That's not who I am anymore! Yes, that happened in my past but it will not determine my future. I am somebody of value and substance. I can make right choices for me and my family. Because that happened in my parents life, it doesn't mean it will happen to me or my kids. I will change my future in my "NOWS".

That's right, talk to yourself,

"That's not my character anymore. That person is "NOW" dead and the things that happened are only found in the past my life. Those things are not in the future of "NOW". Because of my choices in the NOW, my future WILL be different. I choose life and I choose purpose. God has a plan for my life and I choose to find it and fulfill it."

Isaiah 48:17-18 says this, *"The lord, your Redeemer, the Holy One of Israel, says I am the Lord your God, who punishes you for your own good and leads you along the paths that you should follow. Oh, that you had listened to my laws! Then you would have had peace flowing like a gentle river, and great waves of righteousness."* In other words, God was telling me to make a decision that would change my life forever or stay on the path of destruction.

God cannot heal what you won't reveal

Yes, you can choose to stay in a state of self hate, unforgiveness, angry, and bitterness which leads to destruction. It was so very hard to see my future filled with hopes and promises from God. All I could see was this mountain of pain from my past, sitting in my living room as an unwanted guest that would never leave me alone. Yes, I spoke to it, cried over it, quoted scriptures, got into prayer lines, used butter flavored Crisco when I couldn't find my oil one day, and went to counseling. I tried everything I could think of and some things I won't mention. Still, that mountain from my past just got bigger and bigger over the years of my life. The truth is, I thought I tried everything. But the one thing I had was the power and the authority to make a decision in "NOW" for a change and **stick with it.**

God had me just where He wanted me to be. I remember telling women this phrase, "What happens when you get sick and tired of being sick and tired......YOU CHANGE". I was "NOW" ready for my change. God told me,*"your faults are right in front of you, so let's talk about them one by one."* Always remember this, you cannot change, what you aren't willing to confront.... God can't heal what you conceal. So start with revealing your faults to the father, one by one.

First, what is a **fault**? The dictionary says **it is moral weakness, failing, imperfection, shortcoming in character, proneness to yield to temptation, often hidden defect that may cause failure under stress, faulty**. How could the word FAULT describe the years of my life in such details. That led me to look up the word lasciviousness. After the word blew my mind, this is what I got out of it. The word lasciviousness means: **lacking moral and spiritual discipline or restraints, having no regard for accepted rules or standards, from God or man.** God then reminded me of something He told me some time back, "*It is not man's flaws that causes him to fall, it is his faults*". He went on to explain to me the different between the two. A fault is an explanation or a justification why you are the way you are and **refuse to change.** You know, when we say things like;

Because of my mother/ father, I am the way I am....

If I had a good father or mother growing up, I would not be this way...

If I could only get someone to help me with my........

You don't know my childhood....

My husband/wife left me with nothing..........

I was abused by my......

If they had not turned me down for the job...

All faults or things we "REFUSE TO CHANGE" and we have a justification as to why we are the way we are. So start bringing your faults to the father and leave the excuses behind.

take your faults and flaws to the father

While both faults and flaws mean something is wrong, there is a major difference. A **flaw** starts with **you**. A **flaw** is

An admission of ones' weaknesses.

To acknowledge one's character imperfections.

A flaw is accepting responsibility for the wrongs that we have done in our lifetime. But the emphasis is on **you**. Just because an item has a FLAW in it, it doesn't mean it has lost all its value or its usefulness. NOW, God had my attention and my spirit felt true freedom for the first time in years. Yes, I was in tremendous pain. Creflo Dollar said something that touched my spirit, **"PAIN is an intense thought not dealt with."** I didn't want to go back and dig up anything from my past. It took me this long just to forget some of the catastrophic brokenness in my life. But I realized I was interconnected and bound to my past. I had no faith in my future. I lost Tangela on the way to my life and pain showed up. I couldn't quite remember where I left her lying and bleeding to death. NOW God wanted me to think about it again. It was time for me to reveal it to the Father.

God then told me this, "I healeth the broken in heart, and bindeth up their wounds" (Psalms 147:3). There were things in my life I refused to take responsibility for. The battle of wills was on. It was my will against God's. God's trying to take me into "NOW" and my will wanting to stay in the past so I could continue to justify my actions. My past became a place where I could hide from taking responsibility. I could no longer hide behind the reasons why loved ones, friends, and coworkers continue to hurt me over and over again. I asked God, "Why does this keep happening to me?" He answered simply, "You refuse to stay in my presence and become healed." Regardless if I was hurt in the past or maybe hurt in the future, He can heal me NOW, as long as I am in His presence. The choice is yours. You can only operate in the POWER of NOW in your life and reach your destiny IF you stay in His presence. It's NOW time.........

The Infamous Bikini Run

Peeple from all walks of life would stop me. Some I knew personally and others I would have just met that day. They would stop me or my husband or the both of us while we were vacationing in Tucson Arizona. They would stop us to ask the number one question, "WHY? Why did you run in your BIKINI on the Oprah Show?" When my family and I attended TD Jakes Megafest in Atlanta, (both years) people would recognize us there also and ask the same question. We travel a lot for our business and our ministry. At restaurants where we ate when we traveled, people would come up and ask, "Are you that lady that ran in her bikini on the Oprah Show?" In a mall in Panama City, Florida where we went to conferences under our church covering, (Fellowship Church of Praise, Pastors David and Vernette Rosier) people were surprised to see us there. At the military Commissaries and Main Exchanges on Air force bases and Army Posts, people began to tell me how proud they were of me. At the

CHAPTER TWENTY-ONE

YMCA'S where I work out if I'm not at the base gym on Langley Air Force Base Va., people there still keep me encouraged about maintaining my weight lost and my self esteem. Sometimes while I was standing in bank lines or at the teller's window, they also wanted to know the **why** behind the Bikini Run. Grocery stores and Walmart weren't off limits; while they were shopping for the family they were asking me the **why** behind the infamous run. It's been the number one question for me, even to this day.

My job at Ben Franklin Crafts where I am a floral designer, people who recognize me are still asking me about the infamous bikini run. The places where I go and get my hair done, I am still the buzz talk in the shop after all these years. They ask me questions like, "Have you heard from Oprah lately?" I would say, "No, but I'm still waiting patiently to be on her Christmas show. the one she does about her favorite things." Then the whole room is filled with laugher. My friends and neighbors would tell me each year when the Oprah Show replayed my segment. People were so excited to know someone who had been on her show. Then they would explain how that one segment once again inspired them to be free from low self images. They would tell me how that one show reminds them that freedom is a gift that must be used wisely and not left on a shelf somewhere in your life. We would discuss how freedom should be used as a tool to achieve destiny and purpose in our lifetime.

I remember going to a Martin Luther King luncheon with over 200 people at my husband's job and just before the prestigious speaker was introduced, they introduced me. They introduced me as the lady who had the most self- esteem in the entire room and maybe the whole city. It was quite a statement to make about me just from running around in a bikini.

A "TIME FOR MOTHERS" is a conference that comes once a year. They have asked me to speak at their conference each year since the show first aired. The conference is all about women, mothers, and wives remembering the need to nurture their body, mind, and soul. The many speaking engagements I have taken part in have given me an opportunity to tell a little more of the **why** behind my story. Time was still a major factor in how much of my story I could speak about. I left so many women crying in the conferences where I spoke. It left me with the feeling that I must tell the whole story from beginning to the end so healing can began for so many other women. The women were finding me no matter where I was in this world. They wanted to ask me the *whys* and *how's*. They wanted to know about living in their NOWS. They were curious about the NOWS in their lives and how the spirit of freedom can be a way of life for them too.

men asked my husband "why and how?"

On the other hand, the men who loved their women were and still are finding and talking to my husband. They came in droves to his office once they knew where to find him in Chesapeake, VA. My husband Caleb works for the City of Chesapeake. In the daily workings of his job and his years in the USAF, he has established many relationships with companies from all over the world. For the past 25 years with both jobs, he has established some personal and intimate relationships with many of the companies because of his love for people. He was also stopped because they recognized him from the shows that aired. Men were curious to his response to his wife's celebrity status. They wanted to know how he **really felt** about her running in a bikini on national TV. Caleb expressed how he always thought his wife was beautiful and attractive but she did not feel that way. He explained to them how men who truly love their wives, overlook some of the physical flaws their wives stumble over about their physical appearance. He would tell them, "I was so proud of her because she has never been a quitter and this was what she needed to free her. I love it!" Some men would break down in tears and ask, "How did you stay with her all those years? How did you deal with all that because my ex-wife was just like her and it ruined my marriage?" Some would sit down in tears and say, " I love my wife but I cannot reach her any longer. I saw your wife and it gave me hope." These men were policemen, firemen, mechanics, electricians, computer specialist, laborers, supervisors, managers, and men from all different walks of life. They were old, young, black, white, rich, poor and they all wanted to know, "How did you love her thru all of this? What got you thru it all man?"

Caleb would come home and tell me the many stories of him taking guys to lunch or stopping his work for a few minutes to encourage them. He gave up his lunch breaks and time after work to answer their many questions. Many men are still amazed at our marriage and seek us out for counseling. My husband reminds everyone that he had to learn "on the job" because neither of us had a roadmap on how to deal with each other. Caleb is a very transparent person when dealing with men so he still tells of the many mistakes he made trying to help me. He told them how he used criticism and negative motivation to help me but it wound up hurting me. He told them how he sought counsel from pastors, friends, and professionals because he knew there was an answer somewhere. The men are still asking him how he did it and he still maintains, "God showed me because I kept asking God for his help. I just knew I loved her and I refused to give up on her or the marriage. But God had to show me my flaws before I could help her or my family." The men all kept telling him about their wives lack of self esteem and he would keep reminding them to focus on themselves and what they could do to improve themselves first. He reminded them, "you can only change you and cover your wife." As he talked with the many men in his office and on the phone, it was clear that many of the men were disconnected from their wives, their families and true life. The one thing that was consistent was the men crying and crying out for help. They saw my bikini run and appearance on Oprah as a glimmer of hope for them, their wives, and their families.

These and so many other accounts of people asking me or my husband, "Why did you (or your wife) run in a bikini on the Oprah Show for all the world to see you? What is the story behind the Bikini Run?" The people would ask this question knowing they nor I would have enough time to fully explain my emotional state of mind. They all want to know what led to my outburst of freedom that landed me on one of the most famous talk shows of today. After months of trying to explain myself, I decided to sit down with pen in hand and write about the experience.

a life style of change for me

It was in the writing I realized the move of God in my life didn't stop at the four shows my husband and I did, two Oprah shows and two Oprah after the shows. This move was and is a continuous process I *must* complete in my lifetime. It may have started with an e-mail to the Oprah Show, but it has since become a lifestyle of change for me. Remember, ***change is an element in our lives that is indefinite.*** Change can be uncertain, undecided and unpredictable in our lives. The "Infamous Bikini Run" started in my neighborhood, but ended with me running around the world. The run was all about my new found freedom of *change* and the power I found within myself.

Change has no time restraints on it. Change begins in eternity and ends somewhere in infinity. Even after our last breath leaves our body, change is still present. We leave from what is known to the unknown. There is also no interruption in change when it proceeds through our lives. When change knocks on our door, we have only two responses to it. **Yes**, I except change and the responsibility that will come with it: or **No,** I will stay the same and continue with what **I think** change is. Change can be bad or good; the choice will always be in your hands. So take the time that is needed to make the right choice of change in your life. On the Dr. Phil Show, he offers a new change to each and every person who may want it. A person who may say "no" on his show to the possibility of a new change gets the same reply from him every time. "So how is that working for you or why won't you change for the better?" This is the question that everyone should ask themselves. If the answer is ***no*** to a better change, then one must examine someone greater than oneself to find out <u>why</u> he or she won't **change**.

Chapter 22

I am my sister's keeper

Change can be as subtle as a tear drop. I saw the unspoken words of a tear drop in so many women's eyes. Even the women who dared to ask me the *why* behind the infamous bikini run had some unspoken words deep from within. Some of them asked just to know, but others asked hoping to receive the keys to unlock their spirit. The women's unvoiced cries were deafening to my inner ear as I held on to some of their hands. We would stand crying together. They no longer knew how to ask for the assistance they needed. But I could hear their cries in the silence of one tear drop that fell slowly from their faces. Freedom to some of the women was just a dream of what could happen. If only I or someone would care enough to explain how to free *themselves from themselves*. Some of us may *not* like the Oprah Show or even what I did on the show, but God is not **prejudice** about who **He** chooses to use to be a source of help to the nations. You are not perfect and He uses you sometimes! When you become one step above road kill on life's highways like I was, you could care less about where the help comes from. People in that state of mind tend **not** to care about the hand that is assisting them on the road of recovery. We are taking the ride down the road of life and our words can be a deadly drive by to our soul.

Our words can quietly kill us and bring on a slow death while our loved ones watch us, not knowing what to do. Hell's hands can slowly come in and take away our spirit one thought at a time. This death leaves only a shell of what use to be. This cry for help is what I was seeing in some of my sisters' eyes. When the women would look at me, their eyes went pass my flesh and connected with these words: **"I am my sister's keeper."** They were seeing the manifestation of change in my life and dared themselves to want it too. I could see the window of their soul starting to trust me enough to open up. Every word I released became new hope. Maybe this time, they will be able to come out and stay out. They wanted to be free from their self-built strong holds of their own minds. I would begin to try to explain my life changing process to them, but *time* would come in and not let me plant the seed of hope firmly into their hearts. I left frustrated because I knew it would take more time than we had to deposit the spirit of hope into their being. I would quickly write down my name and phone number hoping they would call or write me. Sadly enough, I knew I would never hear from many of them again.

Why didn't I call or write them? That's a very good question. The reason why I didn't call or write them is because I knew they had to make the first move or there wouldn't be a change. How many times have we wanted a change for a friend, more than the friend who needed it? Change is a choice that must be made from a willing heart and mind or change won't happen. People who are in a state of denial must make the first move in order for the right change to work in their life. They must want it more than staying the way they are. Someone told me this powerful statement, *"If you want something you never had, then you must do something you've never done."* **CHANGE**!

the why behind the run

Let's talk about first things first. Why did a plus size African America woman put on a bikini and run through her neighborhood? Why was she waving her hands at people in cars and knocking on her neighbor doors? Why was she telling them of her new found freedom about life itself? If you have read through the chapters of my life *change* in this book, you *now* have a greater understanding of why I would do something that was out of my character. This was the grand finale; the Big Tamale; the last stop into my "NOW"! And what a step it was. I still blush from the very thought of running through my neighborhood with a bikini on. I see my neighbors and think what are they really thinking of me NOW. But my prayers were answered during that bikini run.

I remember the many times I prayed the prayer of Jabez, *"Oh bless me indeed and enlarge my territory that your hand would be with me; keep me from all evil, that I may not cause pain, the lord heard me and granted my prayer."* After reading the book of Jabez, it also altered my way of life. This simple prayer became a part of my spirit and it fed my hopes and dreams. I would ask God, "How can I bless His people with my life?" I prayed for years that God would enlarge my territory to help other hurting women. I wanted to help them find their way out of the maze of low self esteem and not being good enough at work or at home. When the truth of who we are can be manipulated, then a lie can be formed. I wanted to find a way to stop the self hatred when women looked into a mirror and saw a real image of themselves. I desperately wanted to give them something to reach for when they saw themselves.

life is all about choices

It's amazing the things we reach for to hide behind when we see ourselves. If you are a food abuser who thinks food is your only friend, don't be fooled like I was. The food can turn on you and it becomes the weight you carry in silent shame. I wanted to reach the drug abuser. Reach out to the abuser who lifts up drugs far above the throne of God. Once they become hooked on the drug, then the user worships the drug of their choice with all of their emotions, passion and substance for life. This leaves the drug abuser wanting death more than life because of the choices they have made. What about the woman who had an abortion and is still dealing with the feelings of guilt? Who will be there to hold her hands? I can go on and on with the stories about the women I have met in my life's travels. I have cried with them and they have cried with me. I have listened to their stories and prayed that God would bring about a *NOW* change in their life or a place of new beginning. I knew some of them were reaching out for something. Some have received their now and they are working through the process of change. While others are still waiting for a change to come, I would try to leave them with this statement of truth after learning it the hard way for many years, *"Life is all about choice; what you choose in life is what you will have."*

A year and a half before knowing I would be on the Oprah Show, my husband and I came up with a financial plan that would give me an opportunity to come home from working a job for a while. We had to do something because I was burnt out from retail management and life in general. He was missing a wife, friend, and a lover who couldn't find her way back home. I was in need of help and healing from God. My kids gave up on the thought of having the mother they once knew that was full of fun and excitement. My kids began to settle for a M.M.I.A. (Mother Missing In Action). I began to meet all their needs with money. Money I had, but time I didn't have. The love I gave only came after I got some rest. If they needed to go some where, I would pay for someone's gas to take them and pick them up if my husband or I couldn't do it. If food needed to be cooked, cereal, pot pies, TV dinners and hot dogs were my friends. Home cooked meals were few and far between. If the family got a home cooked meal, it was from my husband or my daughter. I might have tried to cook something on my days off but not often. I was in a survival mode and food for them was just another need.

I was choosing change

I did not have time for life because I was burnt out. If my kids needed clothes for school, my husband would bring them to my job and I would put the clothes on layaway only after they picked them out. If I didn't do that, I would get off from work at six and try to go to all the places in one night. I remember my daughter's first prom night. She wore a black and white evening gown with white satin gloves that went to up her elbows. I couldn't be there to dress my beautiful princess. She dressed herself and came by the store where I was working so I could show her off to my employees and co-workers. I took lots of pictures at the store and I tried to make her feel like the beautiful young woman I knew she would grow up to be. What she didn't know was, I was dying inside because I wanted so much to be at home to dress and pamper my little princess. She was growing into a lady right before my eyes. When she left the store, I wanted so badly to go find the pillow aisle and cry for hours. But, I couldn't cry my eyes out because there was a job that needed to be done and employees who needed a supervisor. They did not need a mother who was an emotional wreck. I did like so many other mothers do who have to work. I buried the pain of not being there for my daughter in my soul and a small part of me became numb to the pain. I had to make a choice and I did not like the choices I was picking from.

We decided to bring me home for a while and I was so thankful because I was just surviving in the corporate world. In my year and half of being home, I found my passion for making African art with my hands. Poetry flowed from my spirit onto the paper and the paper seemed to clap as I wrote the music of my heart. It was like a dam of self expression burst inside of me and I found the words to my voice again. It was as if my mind had so much to say that my fingers could not keep up with my mind. My fingers were so happy to write with the passion of love again. My hands would look for the right ink pen and paper to absorb my written expressions. The sun seemed to kiss me in the morning as I arose to go to the bathroom. The kiss of the sun was as soft as the lips of my morning kiss from my husband before leaving to work, a habit we have kept for years. I heard the birds greeting me into a new "NOW" and the clouds shaded any area of shame that I hadn't discovered yet. Oh yes, it was already a blessed day to be alive because I was awakened. I found time in my day to sit in the unspoken presence of God and I was overwhelmed by the deafening of His silence. The dimension I found myself in was spectacular to my ears.

Chapter 23

"Change isn't change until you change."

My son would come in from school and take time to find me in the house no matter where I was or what I was doing. He just wanted to announce his presence to me and tell me all about his day. One of my greatest moments while I was at home, was my son's friends would ask him if his mother would like to come out and play badminton in the back yard with them. The answer was "**yes**" and my heart smiled because I had time to play. My daughter also found a mother who didn't mind cooking, washing clothes and releasing her and her brother from some of the housework. My new statement was **"Moms home NOW."** I had time and energy to talk and teach my children about life and the changes that were going on in their bodies. By now, my son was in the 7th grade and my daughter was a freshman in college. They were both in the midst of life's transitions, adolescence and beginning adulthood. They needed their parent's full attention to understand themselves. Family life was back in the Pierce's home again.

My relationship with my husband still needed some work, but the fire was burning once again in the Pierce's Palace. I wasn't too exhausted and worn-out by the end of my day anymore. I, too, started to look forward to a release from life later on with him. I allowed myself to feel the touch of my husband in the deepest parts of my body. I started to unfold and expose layers of hurt and pain to his many strokes, and it felt so good. We began to cry in each others arms after performing our intimate act of love. Each time we came together to create love, we found love. God then asked me this question, *"How many times can you fall in love with your spouse?"* I told my Father, I don't know the answer to that. There were so many times I stop liking my husband for years. I loved him back then, but I didn't like him. You're asking me how can you love and dislike or hate someone at the same time?

Unfortunately loving someone and disliking them is done in a lot of marriages. Some are evening hating their spouses. I have learned how the liking of a spouse can leave a marriage and then one, if not both of the spouses usually follow the *like* when it leaves. T. D. Jakes said this about men walking out, *"A man can leave a woman he loves, it happens all the time in separations and divorces."* When a man is disrespected over and over again by their women, wives or mother he loves, he can turn and walk away. I heard these words from a preacher that is so true. *"Love is blind, but marriage is an eye opener."* My eyes were opened to what to do and what not to do in my marriage. If I was choosing change, I must make sure it was a godly change and not just a good change. We all have good intentions that sometimes leads to bad decisions. I was falling in love with my spouse all over again because of the NOW I was choosing to stay in.

a broken heart leaks issues

I wanted our marriage to work and to be a testimony. I wanted others to know that if you put God first and put your past behind you, God can heal the marriage and it will work. My Father replied to the question how many times can you fall in love with your spouse with this answer, *"As many times as you are willing to **re-discover** the hidden treasures of their life."* After hearing those words from my Father, forgiveness began to be as natural as the air I breathed. With that same breath, we can release the sins of yesterday's hurts. Caleb and I found healing once again in each other's arms. T. D. Jakes said this truth about a damaged heart and unforgiveness, *"A broken heart leaks issues"* and *"What you won't forgive, you give."* My husband and I were leaking all over each other and our children.

Our children were suffering from the leakage of our flaws and iniquities that we refused to let go. It was the little foxes that were spoiling the vine of our relationship and our home. We apologized to our children and then **changed.** Creflo Dollar made this statement, **"Change isn't change until you change**.*"* Stop talking about change and just make the change that is needed to bring healing to your home. Unless something changes, your heart will continue to leak your issues from the past.

Oprah said this statement on her show many years ago and I have found it to be true. *"We are addicted to the person who best deals with our past."* I was addicted to my husband and the life I knew we could have. If we could only get help to get past ourselves. I was stuck in a world of make believe. I kept trying desperately to make myself believe everything is alright. I was continually telling myself everyone has problems in their marriages so I shouldn't think it is strange in mine. That answer didn't fix the NOW I was in and I refused to accept it anymore. I needed and was looking for a practical and sensible way to reclaim myself and my marriage. I was looking for change.

I had a closed spirit

I found what I was looking for in books and on Christian television. It was there all the time waiting for me to read or to listen to it. Yes, God has all the answers and He is always talking to us. But somewhere in my life, I dialed God's number and then turned off the phone. In my pastor's book, Touched by the Master's Hand by Dr David Rosier, he makes this powerful point revealing why some marriages are ending in divorce. He states, *"I believe on the areas in which we need to get the victory in is selfishness. Jacob had to go through a wrestling with an angel before he was able to change his character."* He goes on to say, *"Before Jacob met with the angel and wrestled with him, he passed over the brook called Jabbok. Jabbok means a place of emptying out."* There was my answer again but I thought I didn't have a place or anyone to talk to. Until one day, I too wrestle with God.

I started asking God, "Where have you been? Why didn't you answer my 911 call?" He replied, *"I did call you back, but you still refuse to make the change."* We all need a place to empty out the harmful words and the toxic thoughts that enter into our everyday lives. My pastor went on to say this in his book on page 71:

"We bring into the marriage anger problems, unforgiveness problems,
past hurts from other relationships that we have not been healed from.
Many have not learned how to work through these issues. We must
learn how to communicate if we are to have successful relationships.
It is impossible to be one without good communication."

This is such an accurate description of my relationship with my husband. I was pulling away from him. Therefore, I took back my words, emotions, and my intimacy and put them under lock and key. I had a closed spirit toward my husband just like my mother has a closed spirit toward my father. I realized I was passing this closed spirit on to future generations.

I did want to pass this down to my daughter or sons. I answered "yes" to change. Change came and I held on to it with all that I had. Going back was not an option I would allow myself to make. I was going to relearn how to unlock my feelings, passion, and closeness toward my husband and family, or die trying. I was saying, Lord I got it NOW!! I knew I would have a testimony and show others how to open their spirit to Change. Now, I can tell and show the world change can be a reality and not just a dream. All of this was being orchestrated by the hand of God. My Father was getting me ready for my famous bikini run. I just didn't know it...........

my dirty little secret

My sister Omegalyn called me like she does from time to time and asked, "Tangela, have you sent your African American Art to Oprah yet?" I said,

"No." But that day when she asked the question, something inside of my spirit leaped. Then I remembered I brought one of Oprah's magazines. The magazine was lying on my dining room table. After talking to my sister, I picked it up to see if there was an address I could send my artwork to. There was no address for sending in artwork. I became puzzled because my spirit wouldn't let me rest about the matter. I said, "God what do you want me to do?" He said, "*Turn on the computer and go to her website and see if you can find something there.*" God fully understood what He was asking me to do.

I didn't know how to turn on any computer, let alone find a website. I hate computers with a passion and I know that goes far past most people's understanding. But yet, God wanted me to do this, so I was obedient to Him. To my surprise, it came on and I found the Oprah Show website without any problems. There is a God! I continued my search for an address to send my beautiful art work. By this time, it had been at least two hours and I got lost in the website. I couldn't find the beginning page and started going into other pages on her website. I went into a site that said if you would like to be on one of the Oprah Shows please write in. I thought to myself and said, "*I haven't done anything great or extraordinary to be on one of her shows. Maybe before I die, God will bless me to do something that would touch the hearts of women or people all over the world. But it won't be today.*" Then I saw a show called "*Stepping Out Your Box.*"

My spirit leaped again and my fingers started to clap. The show was going to be about what is keeping you from achieving your life dreams and desires. God then ask me "*What is it that stops you from selling your African American art all over the world? If I can bless one person in selling African*

American art, I can bless you too. I have no respect of persons." My fingers began to tell the truth about my dirty little secret of shame. I had hidden so well behind my smile for years. I felt free to write the truth because I knew no one would ever read this e-mail. If they did read it, they would **never** call me, so I thought.

I was just a woman with an ordinary life who loves to make gorgeous African American artwork with her hands. The words I was typing were shocking even me on how detailed I was becoming about my life. What I wrote exposed my nakedness. It was the butt naked truth of my deepest thoughts of who I thought I was. I felt no fear while I was writing because I really didn't believe or cared if this e-mail would be read or not. I was writing for the right to be heard and to release my spirit into a dimension of freedom I only dared to dream about.

I was dreaming of my personal freedom. That is why I put this statement into the e-mail to the show, *"If I could run naked or in a two piece bathing suit through my neighborhood, it would free me from this obsession about my weight. Then I could be all that God created me to be"*. At this point in time, my husband came home from work while I was on the computer. He was very suspicious to see me on the computer and he asked me, *"What are you doing?"* I said, *"I'm writing to the Oprah Show about my African American Art."* He started to read the e-mail over my shoulder and we corrected all the grammar errors. At the end of the e-mail, I looked up at him and said *"Do you think I should send it?"* He said, *"Yes, it sounds just like you."* So off went the e-mail to never-never land, never to be heard from again, right?

Chapter 24

The call that changed my life

I sent off the email and went on with life. Four days later I got a call from one of the producers of the show. We had just returned home from church that night. I wanted to check the answering machine for any messages. The voice I heard shocked me. To my surprise, the Oprah show wanted to talk to me about the e-mail I submitted to them. I screamed and I was frozen in time thinking someone heard my silent cry for help......NOW what do I do? Do I dare do what I said I would do.....or back out of it now? I asked God to please help me. His response was very simple. He said, *"Let your yea be yea and your nay be nay."* What my Father was saying was *"Tangela you will have to do this."* Just the thought of the run caused both of my cheeks to blush at once. I called for my husband to come upstairs and I was nervous as I told him to listen to the message. We listened and he started smiling and we were both excited.

A week later, the producer from the Oprah Show showed up with lights, camera and a bikini in hand. The producer brought the bikini with him because it was November and I couldn't find one in my size. I had my sisters in Atlanta, Ga. trying to find me a bikini also. I did not tell all of my sisters the details so they kept asking me why would you need a bikini in November. I said, "Just bring me one, the Oprah Show may need it". It was on and everyone was in place for the showdown. God sent the right producer to His child. The producer God sent was a gentle, giant of a man and he knew and loved my Father too. The producer told me the segment we were shooting will touch the lives of many women all over the world. It all started to make sense and my husband was supporting me every step of the way. The producer explained how the women who will see this segment, will be free from their outer shell of low self-esteem. I knew what I was about to do took a lot of courage but I needed to make the last step to operate in the NOW of my life. I dared not tell anyone but two friends who couldn't make it to the taping at my house. I didn't most people what I had to do. I didn't want them to talk me out of **my first day of freedom for the rest of my life**.

While running through my neighborhood in a bikini, I don't quite remember the moment when liberty embraced me. But it was an empowering act of bravery, not to think or care what people thought about you. I might have been a plus size woman, but my spirit was soaring free above all man made restraints. The producer, who's name I won't mention, said this to me, "Tangela can you please knock on a couple more doors, because this is going to impact the kingdom." So off I went to knock on more of my neighbor's doors. I can't lie to you, half of me wanted to go back home and put some more clothes on. But I knew that going back or stopping the change was no longer an option.

people were laughing and then crying

The final step into my NOW was taking place. I had already spent an hour and a half running in a bikini and knocking on doors. I was headed back home and my husband stopped me and said, "The producer is not done yet, he needs more video." I replied, "Enough is enough. Let's all go back home and finish taping the rest. I am free. I got it now so let's go home." Between my husband and the producer encouraging me with words about freeing women all over the world, I kept going a little longer. With those words of freedom in mind and my wanting to help free others, I stayed almost another hour until all the taping was done. Be careful what you pray for, you might just get it. Now, change had some demands on my life.

The day came when they flew the whole family to Chicago to tape the show with Oprah and the studio audience. When we got to HARPO Studio and after the I.D. checks, I heard these words echoing in the hallway, "*Tangela is here! Tangela is here!*" I thought for a moment, what else do I have to do? Please Lord, don't make me put this bikini on again and run around in front of the studio audience. They wanted me and my family to meet the rest of the senior producers of the show. Then they began to tell me how powerful the segment was going to be. They said the employees at HARPO studio were laughing and then they were crying over my segment. It was replayed over and over in the studio. I was so honored that they would do such a thing. At that moment, I was realizing how powerful a testimony can be in God's hands when it is released to the media.

my father had heard my little cry for help

God was using me to touch people all over the world. The people at the studio kept coming into the green room to tell me and my family how the segment blessed them. Yes, the room it really green. All I could say was, *"Praise Him."* The face of the producer of my segment was beaming with the glory of God. He was so happy about what God was going to do when they released it on that day. The people at the studio were so kind and nice to me and my family. I had made the final leap of change in my life and God had people waiting to celebrate me. My family and I started to feel like celebrities because anything we needed they would get for us. The limousine ride to and from the RAHPO studios was great. The two suites at the Omni hotel along with the food was a blessing too. We took time to go to downtown Chicago. Chicago is beautiful in November with all the Christmas lights and decorations. My family loved visiting Chicago and we still talk about it. I kept smiling because my Father had heard my little cry for help.

My family was experiencing freedom right along with me. The studio sent me to makeup and my family stayed in the green room playing UNO and eating. There were two prayers I prayed before we would do the taping in front of the audience. The first prayer was to meet Oprah before I would see her in the studio. The second was to see the studio before all the people were seated. God granted me my first prayer of meeting Oprah in the green room. This was the segment that wasn't shown. The first time I saw her in person, I felt all the fame and excitement that most people do when they meet someone of her stature. Then God told me to look at her again and tell Him what I saw the second time I looked. This time I looked past the outer shell of fame and fortune. I saw a woman that was no different from someone who understands what to do with the _NOWS_ of her life. I saw a woman with a genuine love for people. I saw some hurts and pains from people words; I saw hurts from people she loved that let her down. I saw the process of God's hands working out the hidden and secretive areas of her life. My spirit was at peace I could sit next to her. NOW, I would not loose my words while others watched and I knew God had heard my prayers again.

My second prayer was answered also. My friend, the producer, said let's go into the studio so I can show you where you will be standing and seating with Oprah. The studio looks smaller in person than on T.V. which was a plus for me. I stopped and looked at every detail of the studio and told myself I will only be talking to three hundred people. Don't worry about the rest of the world; let God handle that part. The feeling of fear began to leave me and I felt my Father's presence of peace. Then it was lights, camera, and action. I was standing behind the studio doors waiting for my cue to come in. I was actually waiting for my heavenly Father to introduce the new Tangela to the rest of the world.

CHAPTER TWENTY-FOUR

God used me to reach other hurting women

There was a small T.V. monitor for me and I was seeing what the world would be seeing of me for the first time. Tears, words that I had no voice to express, began to roll down my cheeks and mess up my makeup. I trusted God through the producer to make my little testimony a voice that could be heard past the low self-esteem that most women would be carrying. The feeling of freedom and independence broke through it's final barrier of my life. My will took wings to fly. The fear of doing the Oprah Show moved over to the NOW I was created to be in. It was my cue to come in. I opened the doors and ran out waving the bikini that represented my grave clothes of what I use to be.

The spirit of living in the NOW was alive and well and I was no longer dead to my life. I was naked and not ashamed with my husband and family by my side. The audience jumped to their feet and the sound of acceptance filled the studio as I ran out to meet Oprah on stage. They told me where I was to stand, but it felt like I was standing on top of the world. My words were flowing just as much as my face was blushing as we talked about my unveiling of my soul. Yes, this was a **now** moment in my life I will never forget. Right after the show, I had another **now** moment with Oprah. When she took my hand while we were back stage after the taping of the show, all I could say was, "*Awesome.*" Oprah then said, "No, you're awesome." I thank God for that *NOW*. Only God can bring the ordinary to the extraordinary and allow the two to meet in the same dimension of time, even if it was for only a brief moment. The "Stepping out of the box" show impact was so great they received thousands of e-mails about my testimony. The producer called me and my husband back in twelve days to meet four of the women who saw the segment that inevitably changed their lives forever. Their new knowledge of the power of NOW gave birth to a new found freedom they never knew they had inside of them. At that moment while standing on the stage with Oprah and listening to the ladies' testimonies how my life changed theirs, a NOW confirmation came from God. It was clear that God was using me to reach other hurting women, and I thank Him with a joyful heart.

Since the first show aired in November 2003, they have shown this segment several times every year. If you would like to see the INFAMOUS BIKINI RUN, go to Oprah.com and pull up her website. Then put my name, Tangela, in the search and I pray that you too will be blessed by watching it.

a thankful heart

I would like to thank the *Oprah Show* and my friend the *producer* for taking a chance on a plus sized woman who had a story to tell. You gave my voice a platform to be heard by millions. Words can not express how much it has changed my life, even to this day. Women who recognize me from the show still tell me their NOW journeys. It couldn't have happened without your support. You will always have a friend in me and in my family.

Also, to the four women I met on the Oprah Show. You four women are the reason why I did what I did. I became naked and not ashamed that

I might bring you four women out. I *still* can't watch the second show without crying. I saw my change reborn again in four other women and it blessed me. Thank you Michelle and I pray you have become the teacher role model you are. Sonya, I still think about you when I workout sometimes and hope you have continue your positive self-image. Remember, it is **not** about a size, it is all about an image. Diets only come to take from you, so try to find a *way of life* that gives you back your life and that more abundantly. This way you will be successful in your weight loss. To Jennifer, please send me a picture and I hope you have plenty of them to send. Don't stop taking pictures of your image because you **are** beautiful to God and those who care about you. To Lisa, have you kept taking out of the clothes that make you feel bad? Remember, lying about yourself in any area is a sign of disapproval and poor self image. You are stunning because there is no one like you.

To the countless other women who are still waiting for me or someone else to help them find their way out of their past and into their NOW, there is still hope. Why? You made a big step because you choose to read this book. Please don't read it just to have said you have read "THE POWER OF *NOW* IN YOUR LIFE". Read this book in the hopes of a beginning, and lasting change for your life.

I would like to dedicate this chapter to the Oprah Show, my producer, and the four women who God used to manifest a dream that came true for me. This was and is only the beginning of my story about the POWER OF NOW IN YOUR LIFE. Look out for the "Power of Now in Your Life, Part II; Now What!"

A journey of change with me

Read and refer back to this book when difficult times find you. You are never alone. Even words can be heard in darkness when spoken to the radiance of God. *Please* bless me with your e-mails or letters telling me how you have discovered your NOW lifestyle. Remember each **NOW** of your life is the hope of a beginning. When you change your life, you change your journey. When your journey is changed, NOW is birthed..........

Talk to Tan

PowerOfNowNtan.com
Or
CalebTan1@aol.com
Tangela B. Pierce
5007C Victory Blvd Suite 159
Yorktown, Va 23693

Bibliography

The King James Version/Amplified Bible Parallel Edition, *Zondervan Publishing House,* 1995.

The Way Living Bible, *Tyndale HousePublishers, 1971.*

Monroe, Myles, *Understanding the Purpose and Power of Prayer,* Whitaker House, 2002.

Rosier, David, *Touched by the Master's Hand,* Morris Publishing, 2005.

The American Heritage Dictionary of the English Language, *Houghton Mifflin Company Publishers, 1976.*

Unless otherwise indicated, all Scripture quotations are from the Holy Bible, *King James Version* of the Bible.

Editorial Note: Even at the cost of violating grammatical rules, we have chosen not to capitalize the name of satan and related names.

Printed in the USA
CPSIA information can be obtained
at www.ICGtesting.com
JSHW012015140824
68134JS00025B/2440